# MARK TIME

JOHN BLAKE

Published by John Blake Publishing Ltd,
3 Bramber Court, 2 Bramber Road,
London W14 9PB, England

www.johnblakepublishing.co.uk

www.facebook.com/johnblakebooks ⬛

twitter.com/jblakebooks ⬛

This edition published in 2015

ISBN: 978 1 78418 644 9

British Library Cataloguing-in-Publication Data:

A catalogue record for this book is available from the British Library.

Design by www.envydesign.co.uk

Printed in Great Britain by CPI Group (UK) Ltd

1 3 5 7 9 10 8 6 4 2

Papers used by John Blake Publishing are natural, recyclable products made
from wood grown in sustainable forests. The manufacturing processes
conform to the environmental regulations of the country of origin.

Every attempt has been made to contact the relevant copyright-holders,
but some were unobtainable. We would be grateful if the
appropriate people could contact us.

# CONTENTS

www.marktimeauthor.com
Twitter: @MarkTimeAuthor
Facebook: Mark Time Author

# AUTHOR'S NOTE

This is a personal reflection on my early years as a Royal Marines recruit. While stories may have been slightly embellished, they are all based on fact or the verbal passing of history through 'dits'. Names, including my own, have been changed to protect the not-so innocent. It is written through the viewpoint of a naïve young man and, while I may now have slightly matured, I thought it important to be true to my young self to illustrate the hardships one must overcome to become the person one seeks to be.

My wholehearted thanks go to the following people for their selfless assistance during the preparation of this book:

John Blake Publishing, for their patient advice and guidance through the minefield of publishing to such a literary sprog.

Andy Screen, the boss at Golden Rivet, for his creative genius in producing the book cover.

Debbie Howarth and the team at the Go Commando charity; you truly define the word 'family'.

Finally, Jo, Connor and Finlay, whose patience, support and unconditional love I hardly deserve.

# FOREWORD

Often, when we thumb through the rows of military books on a retailer's shelf or scroll-through endless internet pages looking for our next e-read, we are overwhelmed by the sheer number of autobiographies of men in the thick of the action.

Some people argue that these publications become a fanfare of self-adulation, written to denigrate anyone possessing human faults apparently absent in the author. This observation, however perceived, should not deny the fact that these writers are true heroes. Those unfortunate enough to have been through the hell of war are most deserved of the respect they receive. If I had endured the same degree of danger, been involved in death-defying acts of heroism or survived the un-survivable, what is to say I wouldn't have written a book in the same vein?

But I didn't. I struggled even to make tea, let alone war. That's because when I joined the military, I was a numpty, an idiot – and a sixteen-year-old idiot at that.

To make matters far worse, I didn't choose to join any old outfit, one where I would occasionally be able to shed my cloak of imbecility. No, my struggles to achieve competence would be tested daily, as not only was I attempting to undertake the longest infantry training in NATO, I was trying to become a Royal Marines Commando.

While many have tried, few have succeeded in gaining the Royal Marines' coveted green beret; even fewer have attempted it when so young, short and scrawny – there is a good reason why, in modern times, the Royal Marines have introduced a minimum bodyweight of 65kg to join.

At age sixteen, many boys are discovering the joys of cheap booze, fags and incessant masturbation. Many retain their commitment to sport – be it football, rugby or mini-golf – and those who can look beyond the sticky pages of a second-hand *Penthouse* magazine may see education as their conduit into adulthood.

I didn't do any of that. I decided to forego the luxury of sleep, comfortable clothing and being indoors during extreme weather, instead choosing a path some said I was neither physically nor mentally ready to tread. Yet as the saying goes, 'The greatest pleasure in life is doing what people say you cannot do.'

This is my journey as a Royal Marines recruit, undertaken as a scraggy, spotty and ludicrously naïve adolescent. It is an account more akin to *The Inbetweeners* than *Bravo Two Zero*, as was my time in basic training. It is a story intentionally written with a stroke of self-effacement, as humility is a highly-regarded trait in the Royal Marines, despite public perception pointing towards an environment full of pouting testosterone.

Some parts of the book may shock those with no connection to the 'Royals'. To those wise in the ways, it will hopefully spark some personal recollection of their own travails during their burgeoning years.

Moreover, while this is a military story, it is inherently a book about spirit, written about a time when life was far more fun, when people did more and offended less; about the spirit instilled in me as a child of sixteen by those green-bereted men.

Like my time in the Corps, this memoir is full of fun, exposing the calamities as well as recognising the greatness. But please – don't expect tales of derring-do. I will leave that to the heroes.

There is little doubt that the Royal Marines are small in number but immense in stature. Formed in 1664, the Corps has developed from a band of 1,200 sea soldiers into an elite modern-day amphibious commando force that is globally revered and feared in equal measure.

There is certainly something in the drinking water at Commando Training Centre, as I have seen at first-hand how the Royal Marines continually produce some of the finest men to grace the shores of the United Kingdom. It may be trifle clichéd, but they truly put the 'Great' into Great Britain.

My time amongst these men was the greatest that a young man could ever wish for, something I probably took for granted at the time. Yet as I ponder the inconsistencies of life through the eyes of middle age, I can look back and glow with pride that for a short, but formative, time, I was a Royal Marine – a 'Bootneck' – and in a way, I still am.

'OARMAARM.'

MARK TIME

# ONE

*'Take me to pleasure town.'*

VERONICA CORNINGSTONE, *ANCHORMAN:*
*THE LEGEND OF RON BURGUNDY*

TAKE A TRAIN journey along the Avocet line from Exeter St
David's to Exmouth in Devon, and in between stops, through
the window to your right, your heart will lift at the green
rolling hills that form a poetic backdrop to the shimmering
Exe Estuary. Boats with witty names like *Sea U Soon* or *Sir
Osis of the River* are either bobbing around their moorings
when the tide is in, or stuck on the mud bank like strawberries
on a cheesecake when the waters retreat.

Look to your left, and you will see the names of the quaint
railway stops that flourished during an era where corseted
ladies carried parasols and dapper gentlemen braved the
estuary wearing hooped bathing suits: Digby and Sowton,
Exton and Polsloe Bridge.

Should you wish to alight at any of these, to soak up the charm of village England, you will see thatched cottages and keen gardeners – most likely named Barbara or Charles – pruning and admiring their floral treasures like proud parents sticking down errant hairs before their child's first day of school.

But not all of the stops on this line are as welcoming. One in particular allows only a certain few to alight. The platform sign could read 'Hell'.

What it actually says is 'Lympstone Commando'.

Behind the barbed wire fencing, huge white rectangular accommodation blocks apparently designed by a sadistic Stalinist architect loom menacingly over a torturous assault course. If you're lucky, you may see green-clad men running, bent over, soaked to the skin, being shouted at quite rudely by white-vested muscle bosuns. For most, this fleeting glance is as close as they will ever get to the realities of life within such a mysterious place. It is the first view of home to those brave enough to take the tentative steps to enter Commando Training Centre Royal Marines (CTCRM), carrying only a suitcase filled with burning ambition to commence their arduous journey to become a Royal Marines Commando.

I took those first steps onto the platform when I was sixteen years and ten days old. My sixteenth birthday present from the government was a train warrant for Lympstone Commando.

The previous weeks of waiting to turn sixteen had been long ones. After passing my initial aptitude tests and interview at the Royal Navy/Royal Marines Careers Office, I completed a medical. I can't recall much about it other than it was the first time I ever had my balls touched. Having it done by an old man who said I had a 'nice physique' isn't how I'd hoped it'd happen. Standing against the height ruler, I measured a smidgeon over the minimum height requirement of 1.64 metres, or 5'4". Luckily, they didn't have a minimum weight requirement in those days, as my weedy 55kg child's body would have definitely failed.

Looking back, I think my obsession with joining up became rather unhealthy. After passing the medical, I'd become so focused on joining that I lost my grip on reality. I was foaming at the mouth to be a Royal Marine. It was like having rabies, but without death or the fear of water. I wanted to join the elite, the commandos, and my pathetic body would have to shape up if I was to succeed.

I secured a job on a not-so-local milk round to get used to waking up during the night, and ran along my route carrying near-frozen bottles of milk as makeshift weights. When I'd finished, before getting changed for school I'd do a hundred press-ups and a hundred sit-ups, then drink my free pint of milk, mixing in a raw egg just like Rocky Balboa.

I used my stepdad's Bullworker to get massive. If it was good enough for Peter Shilton, it was good enough for me. I remember anxiously checking in the mirror to see whether my T-Rex arms had grown. They hadn't. I blamed the Bullworker for not giving me instant results, so I started taking cod liver oil tablets. I'd seen an item on Yorkshire TV's *Calendar* news programme about a champion bodybuilder who consumed them by the handful. But all they did was give me fishy piss to go with my eggy farts. So I started running in my stepdad's pit boots, carrying a 20kg weight in my school haversack – an idea so ridiculous I struggle now to imagine what I was thinking of. I rubbed my shoulders and heels raw, covering them in burns and blisters; ironically these injuries would haunt me during the year ahead.

At this juncture, I think I should add that this spectacularly ill thought-out training regime wasn't even to begin Royal Marines training, but to prepare for the Potential Recruit's Course (PRC).

The PRC is a three-day selection course in which aspiring commandos prove their suitability to commence the full thirty weeks Royal Marines training. Three quarters of applicants don't even make it to the PRC, and I'd managed to be one of the other twenty-five per cent – a statistic I was quite happy to share with friends, repeatedly, until they fell asleep; something I found hard to do the night before first attending.

I'd never been so far away without adult accompaniment, and I found the independence exhilarating. I had two days off school, and watched, entranced, as the Yorkshire countryside's spectrums of green passed by the window of an Intercity train, rather than staring out of my history class window – usually at Dawn, a hot fourth former who sat in an adjacent class. Yet as I steamed further south, the train journey slowly drew me from buoyant excitement to confidence-sinking nerves, as I began to wonder what I was getting myself into.

They say knowledge dispels fear. I'd managed to gain both through watching a video at the recruiting office, reading recruiting pamphlets and eagerly consuming reading material with titles like *Elite Forces*, *Modern Small Arms* and *Razzle*.

I knew the PRC was three days, as it said so on my return ticket. I guessed there would be a lot of shouting and I'd see commandos running around doing commando-like things for the first time. I certainly knew that I wanted to become one of them, or at least I had when sat at home in the comfort of a teenager's bedroom.

Now butterflies churned my stomach, and what I'd eaten got lost in the grimy train toilet that became the therapist with whom I disclosed my tangible fear. What had started out as a *Boy's Own* adventure was quickly turning into a battle for self-belief.

As the looming, white tower blocks of Commando Training Centre came into view, I was in two minds. Would I get off and go through with this madness or take the easy option and remain on the train, another inanimate object passing through to Exmouth? I could tell everyone back home that I missed the connection. They would be none the wiser.

*This must be what it feels like to parachute from a plane,* I remember thinking.

The train stopped. The doors opened. I could hear my heartbeat pump through my chest. My knees felt weak. A few young men alighted. It was now or never.

*Red on.*

I paused.

*Green on.*

Then I followed.

I was surprised at the friendliness of the marine who stood guarding the back gate leading from the Lympstone Commando platform. The corporal in charge didn't shout as much as expected, and we were treated far better than a group of young men who, as we walked past, were running around the nearby drill square with weapons above their heads, directed loudly by an unintelligible instructor. I'd never seen weapons carried like that before, and wondered if it was a sneaky commando method.

We were led to the PRC block away from the rest of the camp. Bunk beds with grey blankets, the smells of polish and the outdoors all stimulated memories of the outward bounds centre I'd visited with my school before trekking over the Yorkshire Dales and conquering Ingleborough, one of the famous Three Peaks. Yet I had the feeling this was going to be no holiday.

I cast my nervous eye around the room and tried to weigh up where I stood in the social pecking order. It didn't take me long to realise I was at the bottom. All the other lads seemed older than me, and they were definitely bigger. One of them even had a moustache! It was with a slight conceit that I noted one lad wore an earring, so I pushed myself one rung up the ladder. Surely people who had ear piercings would never get through? I opened the fluorescent orange PVC sports bag that had served me faithfully through my secondary school years and looked to my side where the bloke next to me, who wore a military-issue jumper, had something I recognised from the recruiting pamphlets. He noticed me looking longingly at it.

'Alright?'

He was the first cockney I had ever met in real life, and he appeared to be far more confident than I.

'Ayup,' I returned, hoping I didn't sound as meek as I felt. 'What's that?'

He then gave that scoffing sound which generally means 'idiot'. '*Pppfff!* Don't you know what it is?'

If I'd been more confident I'd have probably given a rather sarcastic retort, but under the circumstances I just said, 'No.'

'It's webbing. 58 pattern.'

I could have said, 'Webbing? Isn't that on a duck's foot?' Or, '58 pattern? Isn't that something you do with knitting?' Knitting knowledge might have made me sound a little more self-assured. Instead, I said, 'What's it for?'

'It's for carrying all your kit in,' said my new mate. 'Look.'

He opened a couple of the pouches. Inside one I recognised shiny metal mess tins. From the other he unfurled a green roll that contained his toothpaste and toothbrush.

*How very convenient*, I thought, and so much better than the small sandwich bag I'd brought. Storing my toothbrush next to my soap would give cleaning my teeth a rather more carbolic flavour than was ideal.

'Why have you got that?' I said, with honest naivety.

'Why wouldn't I?' he said. 'I'm prepared for anything. Look, I've even got some cord in case my shoelaces break.'

I nodded with feigned awe. Personally, I wore Velcro-strapped trainers.

'I carry it around with me all the time,' he said, airily. 'I'm a sergeant in the Army Cadet Corps. Look.' He turned to show me the three stripes on the right arm of his jumper. I was impressed. The only three stripes I'd ever owned were on my football boots. 'I'm either joining the Royal Marines or the

Parachute Regiment. I can't make up my mind, so I am going for both and then I'm going to pick the best.'

*Wow!* He was the man. He seemed very knowledgeable about all this military malarkey, and it didn't take me long to slip back to the bottom of the pecking order as the communal conversations about military stuff started. I had absolutely no clue about any of it; even the bloke with the earring knew more than me.

I found myself withdrawing into isolation. I didn't want to embarrass myself even more, so I spoke only when spoken to and only about things I knew about, i.e. football and the world's capital cities – a specialty of mine which, in truth, wasn't much use as a conversation piece.

Dinner was a trip into the unknown. The eating hall or 'galley' was a cacophony of cutlery and animalistic devouring of meals, reminding me of my childhood days at Pontins Holiday camps, but with skin headed recruits rather than chain-smoking families. I approached the hotplate. It displayed exotic delights that I'd never seen before. I recognised the sliced beef slapped, limp and forlorn, onto my plate with such force that gravy splattered my one clean shirt. I scooped some oily roast potatoes onto my plate before pondering the culinary conundrum of the other vegetables.

The beef-throwing chef waved his tongs impatiently. As a commando chef he could probably use them as a deadly weapon. On this occasion he just used them as a pointing device. 'You waiting for a bus, Lofty?' he said as I stared into the rack of food.

'Uh, just need some advice.'

'Advice? Do I look like Claire fucking Rayner? Get your scran and piss off, there's a queue behind you.'

I rushed to pick up the tongs that sat in a bunch of unidentifiable green stuff. 'What are these tree things?' I asked the bloke with the earring who stood behind me.

'Tree things?' interrupted the ear-twitching chef, laughing manically. 'Are you from a fucking orphanage? It's broccoli, numb nuts, full of iron and puts hairs on your chest. So I suggest you get some down your grid. It may even put a brain in your head.'

I didn't dare ask him what the tray of small yellow cube things were.

We spent the evening trying on ill-fitting combat gear for the following day's outdoor activities, and then squeezed into an overly-warm room where we were shown countless videos about the Royal Marines. I'd read in one of my newly-acquired books that this technique was used by the SAS to encourage unsuitable people to fall asleep; so to coin an old Yorkshire phrase, there was no way I was going to let a ferret piss in my lug. Some amateurs did submit to the warmth, and were summarily brought out of their slumber by the sharp-eyed corporal. The eye-testing evening continued as he lectured us on such things as the Royal Marines' Victoria Cross winners and the qualities of a commando.

'There are four qualities that distinguish a commando. Does anyone know what they are?'

A silence followed. I pondered the question. From what I had seen you certainly needed to be up for a laugh, but I didn't have the confidence to say so.

'Quality Street?' said some smart Alec to a paucity of chuckles.

The corporal didn't really see the funny side of it either. Even if the joke was shit, I wondered whether I should cross a sense of humour off my mental list.

'Courage,' said the corporal, thus commencing a discussion on what constituted courage – not in the way Plato's Socrates might have but in the manner of a Royal Marines corporal.

'Determination' was number two. The corporal cheerfully insisted a number of us would lack the determination even to get through the next day, though he admitted he'd be happy to be proved wrong.

Surely a sense of humour would be number three?

No. Number three was 'Unselfishness'. This was something I'd never even considered, but then I was an only child. Yet, as the corporal talked, it was clear to see why it was vitally important within a military environment.

After he finished he looked around for anyone who could name the last quality. During the long pause that ensued, I wanted to put my hand up and blurt out 'a sense of humour', but I didn't want to seem an idiot and found no voice.

'No?' said the corporal, eventually. 'Cheerfulness in the face of adversity. Having a sense of humour!' he said, adding a slightly sinister smile for effect.

*Bollocks!* I could have said that. I *should* have said that. I kicked myself for being too scared to speak up. Obviously, courage was one quality I had yet to acquire.

'Okay lads,' he said, by way of wrapping things up. 'You've all done well to get this far. But on average only one in every sixteen candidates who commence the PRC actually becomes a Royal Marines Commando. The rest can't hack it, usually because they lack one or all of the commando qualities.'

For the next two days these qualities would be tested. We would be put through mental and theoretical tests that I found exceedingly easy, and physical tests that were on the opposite end of the spectrum.

The Physical Training Instructors (PTIs) all seemed to have deep voices when they spoke, and yet they shouted in a distinctly nasal, high-pitched falsetto; while they showed little threatening behaviour, I felt terrified in their presence. The corporal from the previous evening was correct though; around six or seven guys dropped out after the first morning's epic gym session.

The bottom field is visible to anyone who passes by CTC, so I hoped the afternoon session there wouldn't spring any surprises. How wrong could I be? Even the warm-up was as energy sapping as anything I'd yet experienced.

Despite it being near-freezing, the PTI wore only a snow-white vest on his top half. 'Keep moving, fellas,' he yelled, before barking out instructions at high speed. 'No one stands still on the bottom field! Five-second sprint GO! Ten press-ups, ten sit-ups, ten star-jumps, GO! Roll over, roll over, roll over, ten sit-ups, GO! Roll over, roll over, roll over that wall, GO! Back again, not quick enough! Front support position place! That's press-ups to you, fellas. Arms bend and stretch arms, bend and stretch. Ten star-jumps, GO! Hurry up! Not quick enough, that wall, GO!'

And so it continued, a white noise of incomprehensible,

ungrammatical shouting that confused us to the point of doing everything wrong. Some of us were doing press-ups while others were rolling into those who were still doing sit-ups, or tripping up people who were sprinting like headless chickens in no discernible direction.

Knackered by the warm-up, we moved on to the height confidence test. Before us stood a large steel structure with thin wooden planks spanning its length. Not ever having been higher than the climbing frame at primary school, I really didn't know how I'd cope at 7m up. As I stood at the bottom of the ladder ready to climb, I hoped my legs didn't turn to jelly like the lad in front of me.

'Come on you, don't take all day,' shouted the PTI – I hoped at someone else.

'I can't do it, Corporal,' the guy above me shouted. It was the lad who, when not scared shitless halfway up a ladder, wore the earring.

'Can't or won't?' the PTI shouted back.

I don't think he was in a position to respond to such a rhetorical question. He just stood transfixed on the ladder, his knuckles white from his vice-like grip.

'Right, get down. Hurry up!'

The lad slowly made his way down the ladder. With me below him, I hoped he hadn't shit his pants. He was sent over to the PRC corporal and sat down. I doubted he would become a Royal Marine – or a window cleaner, for that matter.

It did nothing for my own confidence, but once I was up there I felt okay, despite having only a narrow plank of bendy wood between me and quadriplegia.

Although I'd thought myself pretty fit – playing sport almost continuously and being able to outrun the police – I'd never felt the pain of cramp. Running up the hill towards the metal gate on the assault course, I felt it for the first time. Initially, I didn't know what it was. I hoped it wasn't some kind of leg AIDS, but I knew it was frigging painful. I managed to finish, wincing with pain, and veered towards a PTI who laughingly pulled me to the floor. He stretched my calves to ease the pain and sent me on my way to warm down. I thought I'd blown my chance. Needing immediate attention after completing the assault course surely meant I wasn't fit enough to pass?

We finished the day's physical exercise by conducting a 200m fireman's carry in less than 90 seconds. Already blasted from the previous exertions, I found it immensely tough going. My overworked thighs screamed, my overexerted lungs screamed and the overexcited PTIs screamed.

Passing the finish line, I fell to the ground totally exhausted. I had never experienced anything so strenuous in all my days. Dragged to my feet, I drew in as much air as my distressed lungs could handle and comforted myself that I'd finished. I couldn't believe it. We set off again to run. Thankfully, my leaden legs only were required to reach the warm-down circle. As I staggered forwards, I glanced around and felt slightly better. Everyone else looked like I felt.

That night, the mood was a little more sombre. Whether people didn't possess the energy to smile or perhaps realised their initial confidence had been misplaced I don't know, but I actually felt good; so good, in fact, that I struck up a conversation with a Northern Irish lad about military affairs.

The following day was more of the same, just in dirtier clothes. We had received no instruction to clean our kit, but ignorance held no sway with the corporal who labelled us a bunch of 'dirty scrotes'. This was a word I'd never heard before, but I immediately took ownership of it. It summed me up perfectly. With his bollocking came another reality check, and the demons of uncertainty came back. All I could do was give my all and hope that it was good enough.

The final morning was spent back down on the bottom field. This time, the assault course was tackled as a group with a large telegraph pole to test teamwork and identify natural leaders in the group. Knowing that unselfishness was one of the Corps qualities, I tried to hold the pole for as long as I could – which turned out to be about five metres before we had to work out how to get it across the first obstacle. My leadership abilities were, up until now, confined to a football field of fellow sixteen-year-olds, so my squeaky voice was hardly going to be taken seriously by guys with facial hair. Encouragement and the odd pathetic attempt at suggestion was all I could muster as we clambered unceremoniously over, under and around the obstacles. I was hoarse upon finishing, so I knew I'd gobbed off sufficiently.

By now, the original thirty-five had been whittled down to twenty-five, the others having gone home after deciding a life in the Royal Marines wasn't for them  – or having had that decision made for them. Those of us remaining were hauled into a room for our final results. Our names were called and we were split into two groups. I looked around my group and counted thirteen of us. The army cadet sergeant wasn't present. I feared the worst. My dream of being a Royal Marines Commando was dashed before it had begun. I was already mentally preparing for failure.

A warrant officer, recognised from standing silently on the sidelines throughout the PRC, entered the room.

'Right then, men, do you all want to know how you got on?' He looked at my bunch, and beamed broadly as he spoke. I could see that he had a sense of humour, alright – a fucking cruel one. 'Well, congratulations. You lot have all passed.'

Surely I had misheard? The collective sigh and the odd yelp of delight indicated I hadn't. My first thoughts were of the army cadet sergeant. How had he not passed? He had webbing, for fuck's sake!

'You have all shown the qualities we were looking for,' continued the warrant officer. 'While some of you may not have been the fittest, you have shown that you have the fortitude to push on when the going gets tough.'

Despite my size and the fact that I didn't understand the word 'fortitude', my energy and commitment had been noted. After eulogising over us a little more, he brought us all back to reality.

'These last couple of days, fellas, will be the easiest days you spend at CTC. When you return, be prepared for eight months of hard, hard graft.'

These words of caution wouldn't even begin to describe what lay in wait. But for now, I hardly heard them. I was in!

I travelled home on the train, floating about three inches above the dirty blue nylon British Rail seats.

From then on, my obsession ramped up a gear: from

slightly weird to completely insane. On the flip side, now that I was assured employment, my schoolwork went downhill. I started playing truant, preferring to go out with my mate who had bought a .22 air rifle. We would walk for miles over the nearby fields, taking pot shots at rabbits and missing. I hoped those pesky Soviets were easier to kill.

I fell from A-grade star to D-grade squib all in the space of a few months, much to the protracted dismay of Mr Steele – a former paratrooper and now my careers teacher, who categorically stated I wouldn't have a cat in hell's chance of becoming a marine as I didn't have the ability to 'shut up', 'pay attention' or 'listen'. I cared not a jot. He could shove academia up his well-oiled derriere. I didn't need 'O' levels to become a commando.

I ditched my girlfriend with the consoling words, 'I haven't got time for you *and* the Marines.' Taking the recently released *Rocky IV* as inspiration, I zoned myself into a Zen-like infatuation with anything even remotely related to the green beret. As a potential Royal Marines Commando, I knew I could easily punch Ivan Drago's square head in.

Unfortunately, only a couple of my closest mates were even remotely interested in my career choice. A few saw the military as just another of Thatcher's tools of oppression, and claimed that soldiers wearing police uniforms had beaten up local striking miners. I doubted this, but hoped that if I was wrong they'd punched the fuck out of my stepdad.

In those days, Noel Edmonds' *Late Late Breakfast Show* was screened on a Saturday evening, sandwiched between *Grandstand* and alcohol consumption. Amongst the many features was a section called 'Give It A Whirl', where a whirly wheel labelled with various stunts would be spun and a member of the public volunteered to take part in whichever was selected. One of the stunts was called 'Per Mare Per Terram' which, as I was now smugly aware, was the Corps' motto 'By Sea, By Land' (and not 'By Horse, By Tram', as the corporal on my PRC had warned). One week, the whirly wheel landed on these legendary words and I grabbed anyone who'd listen to ensure they watched the programme the following Saturday.

Trying to get any self-respecting sixteen-year-old to watch Noel Edmonds was as difficult as a commando test in itself, but on the Monday following the show a few of the lads were awestruck by what they had witnessed. The TV volunteer had gone to CTC for a good gym thrashing (by civilian standards) at the hands of the biggest PTI in the Corps, before being sent off around the route of the endurance course, one of the commando tests. The pain of the volunteer and the muscles of the PTI were enough to impress my mates, who now suddenly took an interest in the world I was going into.

Not wanting to disappoint my new fans, I was happy to regale them with tales of PRC, military discipline and activities such as swearing, shouting and painting stones white ('character building', according to a 1950s comedy film about National Service I'd seen somewhere). Going for even more popularity, I lied that nearly all the Royal Marines I'd seen on my PRC were covered in tattoos, which proved their toughness – this was the 1980s, after all, a time when tattoos were usually worn only by military men, miners and prostitutes.

In my area, local teenagers were obsessed with decorating

their arms with as much ink as possible to further their own reputations. Those with working parents had it done professionally. I once watched a mate of mine attending a tattooist in Leeds who would ink anyone who could walk upright; I swear to God the lad who left the chair before him, with a Leeds United badge around his stick-thin shoulder, was twelve. Lads with less disposable income settled either for a pot of Indian ink, needles and a mirror, or went to see a bloke in Ferrybridge who dreamt of one day becoming a tattooist. His artwork, to be fair, wasn't too bad, but his spelling was the sticking point. One lad I played football with had 'bansley FC' on his arm.

I had no tattoos, so those people who'd seen the programme and shown any interest – and who had seen my running improve as dramatically as my swearing and shouting – remained doubtful as to whether I could pass training, due to my virginal skin.

The Arnold Schwarzenegger film *Commando* had just been released, along with Stan Ridgway's song 'Camouflage', in which he sang about a 'big marine'; clearly, if I were to convince the dubious I also needed to put on a bit more bulk. The mirror in my bedroom didn't lie.

Instead of spending what money I had on designer casuals (size XS) for Leeds matches, I bought a 50kg weight set and created a makeshift gymnasium amidst the coal dust of our cellar, and there I spent most of my after-school hours. Given the incessant clunking and banging that emanated from the bowels of the house, accompanied by a range of anguished screams, grunts, and groans, I imagine it was like living with

Fred West. I used U2 albums as my workout music; the irony of training for the British military by squatting to 'Sunday Bloody Sunday' was totally lost on me; I'd run on the spot in our pile of coal to simulate running on a beach, just in case we had to storm Normandy again.

Toughness of mind, and of spirit, was as important as toughness of body. I'd lately watched a BBC documentary series called *Behind the Lines* about Royal Marines mountain leader training, and decided to recreate the cold and misery I'd seen on the show by sleeping in my mate's shed wrapped in plastic bags. I also asked him to hit me with a cricket bat while trapped in a sleeping bag to prove to myself I could endure pain. I even starved myself for two days in a stupid urban survival exercise, turning down the offer of my favourite Findus crispy pancakes from my confused mother.

I knew about cold, I knew about pain and I could resist crispy pancakes.

I was ready.

Some might say for the nuthouse.

# TWO

*'Britain... Thatcher's bloody Britain!'*
RICK, *THE YOUNG ONES*

THE MILITARY WAS never my first choice of career. I had originally wanted to become a geologist.

But the last three years had been difficult, living with my mum and stepdad; my already weak relationship with him became ever more so when I exerted my independence as a sixteen-year-old. The only thing I really wanted to do was see the back of him and, to an extent, my apathetic mother.

Prior to that, my grandparents raised me. The first memory I can picture, through the blur of tears and the feeling of snot running into my crying mouth, is my grandad. In his hand he is holding a clump of hair attached to the scalp of a strange woman who screams as he bashes her head repeatedly against the lime-green dining-room wall, punctuating the thuds by yelling into her face that she is not fit to be a mother.

Maybe she isn't. My gran said she drank too much and was, in her words, a 'racy lady'.

Grandad's enraged attack ends in him dragging the racy lady by her hair to the door and throwing her outside. Inside, the house is silent. Outside, from the side yard, all I can hear is the dreadful sobbing of this strange woman crippled by anguish. I cannot remember how long it was until I saw her again. Her name was June. It took a long time for me to call her 'Mam'.

My grandparents were typical Yorkshire folk – hard, weathered, and they didn't suffer fools gladly. My grandad had never missed a day's work down the pit in his life, other than when he was on strike. But smiling, it seemed, was a luxury he could ill-afford. His life revolved around the colliery and the Labour Club, and his Sunday afternoons were always spent in bed sleeping off his lunchtime booze-up. My gran was even tougher. In her youth she would walk to the pit, eight miles there and eight miles back, to deliver my grandad's 'snap' if he forgot it. She'd get back just in time to start tea for him returning from his twelve-hour shift.

It was a household of addiction. With nine kids, including my mum who apparently used the house as a 'chuffing hotel', my gran's time and money was at a premium. Neither was made any easier by her gambling. In the harshest winters of the 1960s, she resorted to burning the garden fence and old pairs of shoes to keep the house warm, as Grandad would sell his free coal to clear his tab at the Labour Club. In the 1970s, the living room of our council house contained a black and white TV hidden behind a continual fug of smoke from unfiltered cigarettes that stained the ceiling yellow. My grandad forever had a Woodbine hanging from his mouth, possibly to rid him of the aftertaste of Vaseline sandwiches he took down the pit every day for 53 years. My gran had her penchant for whisky and sherry (not in the same glass, mind), and showed her class by chain-smoking Senior Service – an altogether more refined fag than the humble Woodbine.

My own addiction was books and atlases. On my eighth birthday I received a *Philip's World Atlas* that I treasured more than life itself. I would often stay up late reading its maps by torchlight, little realising how much time I'd spend doing this later in life. I could recite every capital city of the world by the time I was eight-and-a-half, and would try to impress schoolmates with the name Ouagadougou, the capital of Upper Volta. Equally as absorbing was the red leather-bound *Readers' Digest Great Encyclopaedic Dictionary (Vol III)* that I renamed my 'red bible', and in which I'd read up on such age-appropriate subjects as anatomy and classical architecture.

I would take it to school and play a game with the other kids. At break time, I'd approach one of them and ask, 'What's your surname?'

'Uh… Bugg. Why?'

I'd then open my red bible and, with a licked finger (intellectuals did that when going through books), slowly flick to the chapter entitled 'Surnames and their Meanings', and then look disappointed when that particular name wasn't in my big red book of everything. Keen to prove its value, I'd flick through again, this time to the anatomical section.

'Do you know what a penis is?'

'Yeah, I'm looking at one. Fuck off.'

Despite often getting ignored, my red bible and atlas opened up a Pandora's box of imagination for me, and while others read comics I'd immerse myself in books on Marco Polo and Alexander the Great. I would write stories set in far-off exotic lands and dream of conquering mountains of the Hindu Kush, exploring Afghanistan and Arabia, places I felt an affinity for after watching films such as *Lawrence of Arabia* and, *Carry On up the Khyber*. If my nose wasn't in my precious books, I'd be completing puzzles and IQ tests. I thought of myself as someone who could immediately get into Cambridge University, despite being ten, as I apparently had an IQ over 150. Clearly, if common sense had been measured in a similar way I'd have been placed in a class with others sympathetically labelled 'special'.

My diet as a child was as unconventional as my reading habits. Dinner tended to consist of a cup of sweet, black Camp Coffee; I'd always fantasise about being in the shoes of the Gordon Highlander who adorned the label, drinking his cup in some far-off land. I imagined the Sikh in the picture making the coffee for his sahib, and wondered whether he accidentally dropped fag ash into it, as my gran often did when she made mine.

'Don't worry about it,' she would add, as I peered into the scalding hot water, watching the ash swirl slowly to the bottom. 'It won't kill you.'

Along with the acrid coffee/chicory/ash brew, I'd consume my nightly packet of shop's-own bourbon biscuits. I'd wolf them down and happily scoop out the soggy remains of saturated biscuits and fag ash from the bottom of the cup. This coffee-and-biscuit combo was my sole midweek diet throughout my early childhood, my gran figuring that my free school lunch would provide sufficient nutrition for the day.

On Saturdays, we had Knottingley's finest fish and chips, bought for us from the shop across the road by Aunt Lily who visited religiously with her large brood of kids. I remember vividly how she would place her false teeth on the chip paper as she simultaneously ate her fish and smoked Lambert & Butler cigarettes.

After lunch, all of us would sit to watch the wrestling on *World of Sport*, my gran and aunt manically knitting in metronomic time with the ebb and flow of the action. Should the baddies, Giant Haystacks or Mick McManus, get the upper hand over any of her favourites, my gran's needles would suddenly stop their click-clacking as she leaned forward to look at the telly, bug-eyed, and use the sort of language that at any other time of the week she'd describe as 'rude'.

Once the wrestling finished, the room would fall deathly silent as if a mute button had been pressed on the household. Grandad had to listen intently to the football results while he filled in his pools coupon. If a mouse farted, it would get the belt. If a gnat suppressed a sneeze, it would get the belt. If any of us children so much as audibly exhaled, we would get the belt.

There was no reason for it. Bob Colson, the results

announcer, would always imply the result through his intonation, and we kids could pick up who'd won a given fixture before he'd finished reading it out (either that or we could just look at the results on the screen).

However, this was of no concern to my grandad. One day, after a poor run of around three weeks of not getting belted, I made the mistake of laughing at a fart from my elder cousin. Let's face it, any 10 year old would when they're not supposed to. Even with his belt at the ready, my ten-year-old self was too quick for grandad, eluding his grasp as I ran upstairs. He didn't follow like he usually did. Eventually, holding my breath and listening out for the tell-tale sound of a creaking stair, I peeked out of my bedroom door. No sign. I crept back down the stairs, hoping he wasn't lying in ambush, and returned to the kitchen that was festooned with skinned rabbits hanging from a washing line.

Grandad was sitting on a chair, looking pale – his miner's tattoo, an Indian ink-blue crack caused by a large block of coal falling on his head years earlier – seemed more pronounced than ever. He was rubbing his bald head and breathing deeply. My gran scolded me back upstairs. It was the last time I ever saw grandad. He had suffered a stroke while trying to chase me. He died later that evening.

After his death, our prize-winning garden fell into disrepair and the house seemed to wither with age – as did my gran, who chain-smoked her way through her single-parenting responsibilities with little money but too much pride to ask for help. She'd be up chopping wood for the fire before I rose until I decided, aged eleven, that it should really be my job.

Unfortunately, so was the cleaning up of dog shit that was a trip hazard around the dining room.

The upshot was that I was farmed out between aunts and uncles more often, especially during the school holidays, to alleviate the child-rearing pressures on my gran. I felt like a wartime evacuee when sent to the West Hull villages, and my time spent amongst the greenery of the Yorkshire Wolds opened my eyes to the wonderment of rolling hills, tree climbing and river rafting – all alien pastimes to a kid surviving the concrete jungle. I suddenly felt alive, with fresh air detoxing my lungs, and realised the books I'd been brought up on were just the prologue to real life.

June, or 'Mammy June' as I began to call her, visited more often. She now lived about a mile away, and so would call in on the occasional Friday evening en route to nightshift at the nearby chemical works. There was still not much of a bond between us, but she did seem to take more of an interest in my life and even came to see me play the title role at my primary school production of *Jonah and the Whale*.

I'd visited her just once at her house on a rough council estate, which she shared with her husband Derek – or 'Dekker' as he was known at the pit. Dekker had encouraged me to go out and play with a neighbour's kid who took me to meet his mates. Ironically, given the profession I'd later follow, my new 'mate' got me to stand in the middle of a circle of about ten other youngsters and fight whoever came into it. I'm not talking play fighting either, this was proper 'smash your fucking teeth in' fighting.

After I'd beaten up the first two volunteers, the others were less keen to try their hands. The biggest lad, whose name I will never forget, pushed another small kid into the circle who I also finished off with my increasingly sore fists. By now I was exhausted. I didn't want any more. I hadn't wanted the previous three either, but it had kind of been put upon me.

Seizing on my weakness, the biggest lad, who was probably fourteen or fifteen, ran into the circle and floored me with a flying kick. On the floor, I was defenceless against the horde that all of a sudden wanted to fight. I lay there curled up into a tight ball, getting kicked from every conceivable direction, trying as best as I could to protect my head. A couple got through and soon the metallic taste of blood covered my tongue. The kicking then stopped, leaving me still curled in a ball. I wanted to cry, to burst into tears, but I couldn't. I wouldn't.

The brain is a strange organ when dealing with trauma. Despite what had just happened, all I could feel was the stinging from a fingernail on my left hand that had been kicked loose. I rose slowly to my feet, ignoring the stares and taunts, and hobbled to my mam's house. My mam was out, only Dekker was there. When I told him what had happened, he just shrugged. 'Well,' he said, 'it's a rough estate.'

I pissed blood for the next week, and have had traces of blood in my urine ever since. Believe me, it's a pain when trying to pass an employment medical.

As I entered my teenage years, my mother's influence on my life became more tangible. I'd been streamed into the top class at secondary school and was captain in many of the sports teams. I was playing football at an extremely high level, and had a reputation as someone who could handle himself in a scrap. Yet for all these youthful achievements, my gran was struggling to look after me due to my increasingly errant behavior. My temper was becoming too much for her to cope with; I'd smashed up my bedroom on many occasions through anger at nothing in particular.

Eventually, and without notice, gran was taken from me to a one-bedroomed bungalow on a warden-assisted estate for old folks. I was carted off to live with my mam and stepdad, who had moved themselves from the rough estate into a posh bungalow in an outlying village. Nobody in the family consulted me or considered how I felt – it just happened. An angry thirteen-year-old forced to live with a disinterested mother and a drunken, violent stepdad; it seemed as if I'd secured a part in a soap opera.

As with most soap operas, death eventually featured. Not long after our separation, I was taken to visit gran on a hospice ward. Cancer had ravaged her body until she lay withered to skin and bone in a ward hammock. I didn't know it would be the last time I would ever see her, but I now understand that the look she gave me said that *she* did.

With my gran gone, I needed family. Unfortunately, I didn't find it at home, so mateship became more important. I found that my eight-mile round trip walking to school afforded me plenty of time to get to know other kids. Many of them weren't as academically minded, but a commonality existed, being from coal-mining families, and that connection only grew stronger in March 1984 when the miners' strike began.

We had moved yet again, our regular transience only surpassed by my stepfather's insistence on buying a shit car every six months. We returned to Knottingley, the rundown pit town in West Yorkshire where I'd been brought up. Spending most days either at home or out on the NUM picket lines, my stepdad did little to encourage bonding, although he'd take me to play football as I was talented.

His public face was that of a champion to the miners' cause, but I loathed him. Many a time I'd return from school only to find the kitchen stinking with dirty plates – totally acceptable given his busy day was filled with watching the horse racing and working his way through a bottle of cheap whisky. We'd argue about who was going to do the washing up. I tried using my stack of homework as a get-out, whereas his case would be short and to the point, consisting of a punch-up I'd invariably lose. My record against him read twenty-one fights, zero wins, twenty losses – and, if I'm being kind to myself, one draw - I'd once managed to twat him on the nose.

Yet I supported him and the miners, becoming an outspoken socialist. Knowing everything there is to know about everything, I saw the world through my red-tinted glasses and wholly partisan view of Maggie Thatcher and the Conservative government.

But whichever side of the electoral fence you sat, the miners' strike destroyed our community and the fractures still remain thirty years later. Despite his earlier championing of the cause, my stepdad went back to work before most, so his comradeship with the other miners became a distant memory, resulting in our house being daubed with 'scab'. Even worse, we awoke one morning to find our living room curtains ablaze after someone had set them alight by poking a burning newspaper through the letterbox. Socialism, it seemed, was honourable enough within the pages of *The Guardian*; having some leftwing arsonist trying to set fire to me put me off it for a while. After the strike collapsed, the subsequent months became a festering wound. Once close families drew battle lines over garden fences. Breadwinners saw their dreams of a job for life dashed and the hopes of future generations were put in doubt through the decline of local industry. The Smiths became the soundtrack to disaffected local youths, who chose delinquency over order, blaming anyone who wore a tie for the bleakness they had inherited.

I had to escape this life. I could see it dragging me down.

I decided to turn my life around and knuckle down at school. I was bright enough to be in the same class as a future maths professor, a heart surgeon and an adviser to the Home Secretary (it's not hard to advise politicians, the difficulty seems to lie in getting them to act upon it), but up to then had neglected my academic potential, preferring to drink Woodpecker cider in the park with the lads, go to Leeds United matches and try to start fights with the police. Now I set my sights on going to university and training to be a geologist.

Unfortunately, that meant studying for 'A' levels, and that, in turn, meant stability. But with my stepdad now ostracised by his community, he and my mam were looking for an escape route of their own. I discovered this by coming across 'business for sale' particulars and circled classified ads in mushy pea-covered newspapers. My life was about to take another turn, with the impetus provided by my mother.

'You need to think about leaving home and getting a job,' she said to me one day. 'That will be better for you than that sixth-form rubbish. Here... have a look at these.' And with that she thrust a bunch of army recruiting pamphlets into my fifteen-year-old fist.

I had never had any interest in the military. The Air Force Cadet detachment at my school was enough to put anyone off. Only the metal-mouthed geeks had joined and none of them had cool mates, unlike us geology boffins. But to my surprise, as I pored over the pamphlets I found a genuine interest in something other than football and basalt. The British Army seemed to be an ideal fit for me – mates, travel, sport and a uniform the girls would surely swoon over. And I could join as soon as I left school.

I paid a visit to the Army Recruiting Office, my inquisitiveness equalling my enthusiasm. The recruiting sergeant advised me to sign up as a Construction Materials Technician. He said, rather vaguely, that it was 'like being a geologist in the army'. I have to say he was a very nice man, and very smart – though his clipped moustache made him look a little too much like *Grange Hill*'s Mr Bronson. Nevertheless, I went ahead and took the technicians' aptitude tests. With a ninety-nine per cent pass mark in the bag, I was given the date for my interview. It was with the excitement of a small child on Christmas morning that I exited through the door facing the adjacent Royal Navy Careers Office.

I stopped in my tracks and stared.

The RN had just changed its window display from flares-wearing sailors to Royal Marines Commandos looking like harbingers of death and doing things James Bond might have wet dreams over. I studied the pictures. The word 'Commando' jumped out at me. It was the magnet, the tractor beam that attracted thousands like me every year. So, in a moment of utter insanity, I forgot all about a job that could give me a well-paid lifelong career to take on an occupation that involved killing people and shitting in plastic bags.

Inside, a tubby sailor sat behind a desk. He looked me up and down; given my diminutive stature, he probably thought I was sounding out the vacancy situation for Royal Navy stewards.

'I want to join the Marines,' I said, boldly. Having just passed a technicians' interview, I reasoned I was surely a prize catch.

'Well,' he said, dismissively, 'you'd better go over to America then, son.'

I was flummoxed. I just stood there, not knowing what to say or do. Apparently passing a technician's interview didn't mean you were exempt from looking stupid. Eventually, he spoke for me. 'I take it you mean the *Royal* Marines? There is a difference, you know.'

'Oh,' I said. 'Sorry. Yes.'

'Dave?' he called over his shoulder, and from a backroom appeared a giant of a man with the world's thickest arms. I gulped. Did I really want to join the Marines – sorry, the *Royal* Marines – if they were all like him?

*Fuck, yes.*

'Right you are then, Lofty,' said Dave the giant in a surprisingly soft voice. He pointed to a bar spanning an alcove. 'I'm not going to bother my arse talking to you unless you can do ten pull-ups. You know what a pull-up is?'

I nodded confidently. Of course I did. I watched *Superstars*.

'And it's not like they do it on *Superstars*.'

*Fuck*.

'They do pull-ups underarm,' he said. 'Royal Marines do 'em overarm.'

He grabbed the bar – he didn't need to jump – and demonstrated the grip. Then he paused and gave a sarcastic smile. 'Of course, the ability to actually reach the bar is part of the test.'

Happy with the task ahead, I jumped up and pulled myself up, planting my chin over the bar as instructed. I repeated this manoeuvre again and again and again, and after doing the requisite ten I carried on.

'Alright,' said the giant. 'Get down. No need to show off.'

I giggled in excited relief as my feet hit the deck.

'Good effort,' he said. 'Now I'll talk to you. Come through.'

After our introductions, he asked the ultimate question.

'So, why do you want to join the Royal Marines?'

It was as if he had asked me to explain Einstein's theory of relativity, only with commandos as elementary particles. I was totally stumped. I had popped in on a whim and was totally unprepared.

'Well,' I said. 'I've passed the technicians exam for the army.'

*That should impress him.*

'And?'

*Maybe not.*

'Well, it looks as though the Royal Marines are better.'

'At what?'

'Being commandos?'

*Well done, that's brilliant stuff.*

He paused. 'How much do you know about the Corps, son?'

The *core*? What was he on about? Working on the basis that it must be some sort of alternative name for the Royal Marines, and deciding to come clean, I said, 'Actually, pretty little. I liked the look of the window display.'

*That's it, I've blown it. I'm trying to join the Royal Marines here, not frigging Debenhams.*

'Well, at least you're honest. That's a good start. Integrity is something we seek. We can book you in for the aptitude tests but, to be honest, you need to start reading up on life as a Royal Marine. It's totally different from the army. We wash, for a start.'

Our talk ended with a test date booked, and a handful of pamphlets given out by the sailor. 'Here,' he said, 'have a look at these as well.'

I smiled and thanked him. There was no way I was going to be a matelot. I had been seasick on the pedalos on Bridlington boating lake.

I returned a couple of weeks later to conduct my numeracy, literacy and mechanical aptitude tests. I found them comparatively easy and the maths test was especially pleasing, as no calculus was involved. The adjudicating naval petty officer called me in to his small area once the marks had been completed.

'Listen, son,' he said. 'I've had a look at your marks and

you should be applying for a technician or artificer's job in the Royal Navy. You can read and write... you'll be over-qualified as a booty.'

I listened, but my mind was elsewhere. I was imagining myself as an alpha male, abseiling from helicopters and storming exotic beaches.

I was then interviewed by a Royal Marines warrant officer. This went swimmingly, not least because he too was from a broken home. He waxed lyrical about 'the Corps', as he repeatedly called it, and said more than once, 'It has been my family.'

A family was certainly something I was hankering after – a group of people who would look after me, where I could blossom into someone I could be proud of.

\* \* \*

After passing the PRC, my joining date couldn't come soon enough. Even then it was too long.

As per usual, my stepdad's Friday night consisted of going to the working men's club and getting so drunk he could hardly mutter his name. On one particular occasion, my mother joined him and I was left to look after the puppy they'd just acquired – logical, when you're about to purchase a fish and chip shop.

After yet another gut-churning clean-up of the dog's arse gravy, I stuck on a video of *Gremlins*. Later on, the back door slammed open and I could hear my mother screaming obscenities over the film. She stumbled into the living room, bleeding heavily from the mouth, followed by my stepdad, who stood there glowering. He had punched her full in the face, breaking her two front teeth and splitting her lip.

I didn't know what to do. He'd used me as a punch bag often enough, but this was the first time I'd seen him physically abusing my mam. He launched at her again, grabbing her hair. This time, thirteen years after I'd last seen her in this situation, I could do something. I launched into him with every joule of anger I had, knocking him to the floor.

I thought I'd done a satisfactory job but my fighting ability wasn't really up to his standard. He got up quicker than a drunken arsehole should ever be able to, and grabbed my throat, choking me out with his gargantuan miner's hands. My weight training hadn't prepared me for this. If he'd asked to arm wrestle I might have been able to put up some form of resistance, but he was doing me serious damage.

Just as the stars in my eyes started to be extinguished, his grip loosened as his body crashed to the floor. My mam stood over him, a half-full vodka bottle in her hand. When you get hit over the head with one of those babies they don't smash like they do in the films. He was out for the count. We left that night, but within two days we were back. Strangely enough, he never hit me again.

I tried to keep my distance from then on, and spent a lot of time at my mate Craig's house rather than enduring my stepdad's shit. Craig's mam put me on the straight and narrow once more, insisting I study just in case I got injured and couldn't carry on in the Marines. Of course, this was bollocks. I was invincible; the only thing that might stop me would be nuclear war, but as a Royal Marine I could deal with that too.

Not long after that, my mam and stepdad bought their chippy at Seacroft in northeast Leeds. This was the second biggest council estate in Yorkshire and one of the most impoverished suburbs in England. It made Knottingley seem like Beverly Hills. Kids of eight walked around the estate with a bag of chips in one hand and a bag of glue in the other. Fifty per cent of the grownups seemed to live off a diet of cigarettes and alcohol or, if money was too tight, butane. Those who did eat food chose fish and chips, which made my mam's shop a tidy investment. Thursday was dole day, so the shop would be heaving with punters and their pocketful of benefits. It all strengthened my resolve to leave.

Yet here amidst the litter-strewn streets, burnt-out cars and smashed, piss-stinking phone boxes, rather than poverty being an excuse for failure it nurtured resilience, resourcefulness and ingenuity – all characteristics needed in any walk of life to attain success, and certainly components in building a highly-skilled soldier. It's of little wonder that the council estates of the working classes are the breeding grounds for the UK's continuing military excellence.

My mam and stepdad had timed the move perfectly: the week prior to my first 'O' level exam. I was shunted around from pillar to post, looked after by relatives and friends just so I could actually sit the exams I'd spent the previous eleven years studying for. If there had been an 'O' level in Royal Marines Studies I'd have got an A. Unfortunately, none of the nine I took included the word 'webbing'.

The one good thing about Seacroft – other than the ready availability of glue, should you break a vase – was the park next to our chip shop. Its periphery was littered with benches and other wooden obstacles that wouldn't have seemed out of place on a military assault course. It was ideal prep for the two weeks between my last exam and my joining date on 14 July 1986.

One day, a bloke I'd seen regularly walking his dog while I trained approached me. 'What you up to then, son?' he said, as the dog licked his balls (his own balls, I should add, not the owner's).

'How do you mean?' I said, eyeing him with caution and wondering whether he was the new Yorkshire Ripper.

'Well, you're the on'y daft bastard I've seen running, jumping and scrambling ovver all this lot wi'out a copper chasing you,' he said. 'I just wondered why.'

I explained, and he nodded gravely.

'Chuffing 'ell, tha needs to get some meat on thee bones. I wor' in Paras, mesen. Let me tell you this: when you join an outfit like Royal Marines, think o' hardest thing you could ever do. Then double it.'

# THREE

**'A first visit to a madhouse is always a shock.'**
ANNA FREUD, PSYCHOANALYST

THE SATURDAY NIGHT prior to leaving for Lympstone, I went home to Knottingley to be with my schoolmates. I spent the last of my family allowance drinking more cheap whisky than I care to remember, in derelict pubs that survived on the trade of underage drinkers. I ended the night walking home a girl who, unbeknown to me, had fancied me all the way through school. I was hoping it might lead to my first sexual encounter, but it ended with her giving me a chain of love bites and me stepping in some dog shit - an altogether unsatisfactory end to a potential cherry-popping scenario. Ending up back at my mate Craig's house, his mam watched over me throughout the night as I repeatedly vomited whisky and bile, onto her soon-to-be-ruined sheepskin rug in front of the electric fire.

All the preparation had finally ended. The months of training, the weeks of excitement, the days of trying desperately to lose my virginity before joining up... it had all led up to this.

The day of joining would be the first day of my new life and the last day of the old. It was a momentous occasion, but one that passed my mam and stepdad by. They were too busy filleting fish to take me to the station, though Dekker did at least lend me twenty quid to get the bus to Leeds Central train station and for a bit of spending cash. It was the first and last time I'd ever borrow money from him, and the only money I had to see me through the next fortnight – despite the joining instructions suggesting sufficient cash to buy items necessary for the first two weeks of training.

As the Plymouth-bound Intercity train departed Leeds, I realised there was no turning back, even though I'd forgotten to pack any spare pants. The Exmouth-bound train from Exeter St Davids seemed to have a few smartly-dressed young men on board. I looked at them furtively, from behind an old copy of *Shoot* football magazine. They were either very young businessmen, on their way to court, or, more likely, undertaking the same journey (both literally and figuratively) as I was. This made me feel even more nervous. I felt totally underdressed in my skanky cords, polo shirt and trusty Puma G Vilas trainers (which I'd at least scrubbed for the occasion). I didn't even own a pair of shoes. I certainly didn't own a tie – I'd burnt my school one in a theatrical liberation from educational servitude.

I buried my head back in an interview with Chris Waddle in his ridiculous permed mullet, unsuccessfully trying to ignore my butterflies. They only got worse, and by the time the familiar sight of Lympstone Commando came into view the lack of spare pants was certainly a worry.

Awaiting our arrival was a moustachioed drill instructor (mystifyingly acronymised as 'DL') who would be our father, mother and torturer for the first two weeks of training. I got shouted at even before both feet hit the platform tarmac. I can't recall his exact words, but I think the gist of it was that I evidently had some form of intellectual and physical disability. The shouting wasn't the spit-in-your-face squealing you see in films depicting life in the United States Marine Corps. This was more of a calculated, reasoned raising of the voice, thus even scarier. I have to say it was all a far cry from my PRC, where that polite marine had opened the gate for us.

I desperately tried not to draw any attention to myself, noting to my surprise that the DL had what some personal trainers describe as a 'carb face'. He looked slightly overweight to be a commando, and his chin wobbled as he spoke, but in my youthful naivety I fantasised that he was an injured power-lifting champion.

We lined up on the platform as ordered. He came by each one of us to ask our name and offer some sarcastic comment. The lad next to me was the first to be addressed.

'Name?'

'Andrew Webb.'

'Oh, Andrew is it?' the DL said. 'Do you mind if I call you Andy?'

Andy took this innocently, failing entirely to spot the concealed malice. 'Uh, yep, that's fine.'

'Okay, Andy, this is what happens now: you get your fucking heels together and address me as "Corporal". The day I call you by your first name is the day I like you, and at the moment that's a long fucking way off. Surname only, you fucking scrote. Get it?'

'Yes, Corporal.'

'Name?' He looked me up and down and I felt a little unnerved by even this small exchange. I hoped he wouldn't say 'fucking' more than three times to me.

'Time, Corporal.'

He ticked his paperwork. 'Did you get the joining instructions, Time?'

'Yes, Corporal.'

'So where on the instructions does it say come dressed as a scruffy cunt?'

'It doesn't, Corporal.' Or at least I didn't think it had. I'd read them pretty thoroughly, and I'd have certainly noticed the 'c' word.

'No, it fucking doesn't. It says wear smart clothing. So why have you come dressed as Harold fucking Steptoe?'

'These are my best clothes, Corporal.'

'Fuck me, you don't even own a pair of trousers?'

'No, Corporal.'

'Where you from, Time?'

'Leeds, Corporal.'

'Ah, that would explain it then. Fucking pikey.'

After each one of us offered our name and got roundly abused in return, we picked up our luggage and shunted through the single gate. He organised us into two files, then proceeded to instruct us how to march as best we could weighed down with bags.

'By the left, quick march! *Eft ite, eft ite, eft ite...*'

With my experience of logic puzzles in my mam's *Puzzle Break* magazine, I quickly fathomed his speech impediment was timing our step. I did as best I could, following others who looked nothing like smart guardsmen either. They carried suitcases, sports bags, and one had a half-eaten sandwich hanging from his person.

We were led to a large block with the words 'Induction' above a huge globe and laurel motif, the emblem of the Royal Marines.

Inside a cavernous room was a row of bed frames uniformly spaced around the four walls, each with a single locker at its foot. Searching around, we found the bed with our name alphabetically positioned, mine typically near the entrance to the toilets.

As I had on my PRC, I compared myself to those who were undertaking the same journey. I had yet to say a word to anyone; the guy next to me, who was clearly older, decided to talk to the bloke the other side of him. It was evident we'd find commonality with those of similar age. Unfortunately, there seemed to be few other children for me to talk to.

There was not an earring in sight as I watched people unpacking their meagre belongings. There seemed to be an air of quiet, possibly a nervous exhilaration or shock of capture that affected even the older guys who already had tattoos, scars and filthy vocabulary.

One sweaty lad took off his shirt. Whether this was

to relieve himself from the heat or he just wanted to show off his Apollonian physique, I don't know, but I stared in admiration at his chiselled body, one I'd dreamt of achieving while grunting and groaning in my cellar. He soon became the catalyst for others to follow suit and, before long, half of the group were topless. The more I saw these already-formed muscles and tautly athletic torsos, the more it occurred to me I was physically way behind most of these guys. I would have to catch up quickly.

Before I could pop off to the toilets for some emergency press-ups, the DL caught our attention. 'Listen in, gents,' he said. 'There are now fifty-two of you stood here, a number that I know will drop rather rapidly in the coming weeks. You are now the recruits of 299 Troop, part of Portsmouth Company for the first fifteen weeks of Phase One infantry training.'

Shepherded to an office for administrative processing, we were subjected to more sarcasm by the most frightening looking man on the planet, who had the audacity to be a clerk.

My first name would no longer be 'Mark', but 'PO45739X Junior Marine', which was definitely harder to remember. In fact, I was so concerned about remembering it correctly when reporting to anyone of higher rank – which at this stage of training was anyone inside the perimeter fence, including animal mascots – that I actually struggled to remember my surname.

Most of that first day, the smell of varying cleaning products was never far from my nostrils. I ran around in a confused state, rarely saying anything other than, 'Yes, Corporal.' Seemingly everything we said had to end in the word 'Corporal', drawing the ire of a sergeant in the bedding store when addressed as such by Andy Webb.

'I've got three stripes, you buffoon. That means I'm a sergeant, not a corporal. What am I?' he demanded.

'You're a sergeant, Corporal!' shouted Webb.

We had to be issued with various pieces of bulky equipment, which were hard to carry without looking like an idiot, undergo more paper administration, pledge oaths to the Queen and ensure our joining routine card was complete. The latter was the archaic administrative task ensuring the relevant departments officially recorded our presence by way of an ink stamp, an entry into a ledger and some complaint about interrupting someone's 'stand easy'. It was like a cross between a bingo card and a treasure hunt indicating mysterious departments hidden around camp that we had to find, with our only clue being, 'Get it filled in before the end of the day or you can standby.'

In between, we were summoned to line up with everyone else outside the barber's shop.

'Would anyone like to keep their hair?' said the DL, casually.

One long-haired soul put up his hand. 'Yes, I would, Corporal.'

'Well, have you brought a bag?'

We were each herded inside and given a very brutal haircut by an overly enthusiastic old barber who had clearly trained on sheep.

Finally, we had our photographs taken in the photo booth of lies – transforming me into something from *Crimewatch*, rather than the scared child I actually was.

Before there was any instruction on how to creep up behind the enemy and garrote him with cheese wire, we were ordered to the NAAFI shop to buy specific items we needed for the next couple of weeks. The Navy Army Air Force Institute is the paramilitary arm of consumerism, selling items at extortionate prices to a captive market. The NAAFI at CTC offered a wide range catering to its main demographic: from a cigarette lighter in the shape of various exotic animals, which for some reason wasn't a big seller, to pornography, which was.

Now high on the list of life's necessities were items unknown to most teenage boys: washing powder (dhobi dust), Brasso, Duraglit, whitening fluid for pumps (blanco), nail-scrubbing brush, on/off boot-polish brushes, boot polish, starch and flip-flops. I took one of all of the above, and dumped everything into my newly bought plastic bucket. It left me with 45p to last the rest of the fortnight. The Ferrari could wait.

The military-issue kit was an assortment of clothing and equipment as varied as our pick'n'mix of accents. We were shown once how to launder and look after our issued clothing. As ever, there would be no second demonstration; information had to be absorbed immediately. We wore hessian-like green shirts for normal duties, as opposed to the smooth stone shirts worn for drill. These needed to be as sharp as a pin, but would crease as soon as you looked at them. They would only iron well with the correct amount of starch. Too little starch made no difference. Too much and the subsequent stains looked like the wearer had become sexually excited. Our trousers, known as 'denims' but nothing like jeans, also had to be pressed to the required standard, and 'immaculate' was the only acceptable standard. This required arm-jarring pressing of the legs to create creases so sharp you could shave with them.

On our feet, depending on the activity, we would wear Royal Marine high combat boots (RMHCB), which I loved as they made me at least an inch taller. On the down side, I looked like a glam rocker and they weighed the same as me, so running became especially exhausting. Bearing in mind we ran everywhere, they hardly made me feel like Darren Coe, Seb's faster brother. We were issued two pairs of RMHCB, no doubt so that we could suffer twice as many blisters. Inside, we would insert plastic insoles that shared their moulding with 'ACME Cheese Grater Inc'. Burning and rubbing, rather than cushioning and comforting, seemed to be the design priorities; they were so tough they could only be cleaned by scrubbing them with something equally as abrasive - another insole. The friction caused by rubbing a socked foot against the granite-hard plastic abrasions would be the only thing keeping us warm when winter approached.

Drill boots, or 'boots AP' (achingly painful) as they were known, were the bane of every new recruit's life. It was the first time I ever ironed a pair of boots – to smooth down the toecaps in preparation for the term forever associated with National Service - spit and polish. Shining toecaps to give a mirror finish took time and effort, and those who had the skill could make a few quid as a small-time boot polisher. The method I was shown was to apply a thin layer of polish with a duster or dry cotton wool; the polish then moistened with either some breath, spit or, for us modern types, tap water. Wet cotton wool was then used to smooth to a finish. This was repeated *ad infinitum* like a battery hen eating grain. It was impossible to get these boots 'too polished', and there was no obvious demarcation line between 'not good enough' and 'good enough'. Only the DL would decide that, his opinion determined by his mood. This activity alone could take up a good couple of hours of a new recruit's evening. On my deathbed I will ask the Lord for at least seven days extra, to make up for the time I lost polishing frigging drill boots.

Gym pumps, known as 'daps', were just the adult version of the plimsolls worn by young children. Even these simple pieces of rubber and canvas required as much care and attention as every other bit of kit. After each workout, the cardboard-thin soles had to be scrubbed, the whitening blanco reapplied and the laces washed. Any marks on the gleaming white material stood out like a racing dog's gonads to the beady-eyed PTIs and would result in a hairdryer of a bollocking, accompanied by press-ups or burpees or sit-ups; just what we needed before a long session of press-ups, burpees and sit-ups.

The most significant piece of clothing issued was the beret. Unless we were big fans of Frank Spencer, the chances were that none of us had ever worn one. The Royal Marine recruit beret was dark blue with a red patch at the front, in memory of the beret worn prior to the granting of commando status in 1940. Its shaping was troublesome. Rather than the sleek, moulded beret of our dreams, it often resembled an aircraft carrier's landing deck. On the red patch we punctured two holes, using a ruler for perfect placing of the globe and laurel leaf cap badge of the Corps. Behind the badge sat two protruding pin posts. Between their eyes sat a pin to hold the cap badge firmly in position. These post pins were just long enough to press uncomfortably into the forehead so as to elicit a headache, and just short enough to stick into the forehead when the DL smacked the cap badge into the skull for having it 'slightly out of place'. I still have a small indentation in my head from my careless misplacement.

The field equipment we were issued was a myriad of pouches, sacks and mysterious utensils that would be our life support system out on exercise or operations. To my untrained eye, the various parts looked like an extremely difficult 3D jigsaw puzzle straight from *The Krypton Factor*. I struggled to fathom what went where, watching the corporal like a hawk as he put the items together with *Blue Peter*-type instructions, even having a set he'd prepared earlier. The 58 pattern webbing system, as was issued in those days, had been designed by a woman. As I'd yet to grasp the intricacies of a rear-fastening bra strap, I laboured to see how to fix the various items together. Those who received new webbing, as opposed to cast-offs, were further handicapped by material as flexible as a band of forged steel; you needed the grip of Arnold Schwarzenegger to bend the various buckles, pins and fasteners together.

Streamlined in design, every pouch was designed to hold a certain piece of equipment which was slightly too big to fit comfortably. As I was later to find out on numerous occasions, the pouch would shrink further when wet, just enough to make inserting that certain piece of equipment impossible without a five minute fight of pushing, pulling and swearing.

I marvelled at the scarcity of equipment that would be our field 'home': a sleeping bag that unravelled to the size of a sofa and released the wonderful, musty aroma of damp soil. There was a 'poncho' that was nothing like the Mexican version, but when unravelled became our bivouac shelter or 'bivvy', and also released the wonderful, musty aroma of damp soil. We would sleep on a roll mat, a thin roll of foam that, when unraveled, released the wonderful, musty aroma of (well, I'm sure you can guess...).

Also issued were a water bottle and mug, two mess tins scoured, scratched and scored more than an Olympic ice-skating rink, and a KFS (knife fork spoon) in a luxurious faux-leather case. In addition, we were given a holdall to be filled with a three-piece razor and ten blades, a soap, a flannel, a housekeeping needle and thread, 20m of green string, a metal mirror, the KFS, boot polish and brush, comb, toothbrush and toothpaste. The holdall could accommodate a quarter of these items at best, but it grew from the size of an immature courgette when empty to that of a steroid-infused marrow. Of course, it then had to fit inside a pouch the size of an aubergine with muscular dystrophy.

I was happy to be issued a pick rather than a shovel. It looked easier to pack, and I'd hated shovelling the garden beds as a boy when press-ganged into helping my grandad tend to his prize-winning roses. Also, I reckoned the ergonomic benefits of the pick would be a godsend when it came to actually using it. Surely gravity would assist the downward force of a pick, whereas a shovel needed strength applied to lift things up? On the other hand, carrying a pick over my shoulder would make me look like one of the seven dwarves, hopefully not Dopey (although he wore the most stylish hat).

Near the end of day one, the timetable listed a 'washing demonstration'. Even I felt a little patronised to be told how to wash. I was clean; I had my *Lynx* deodorant to prove it. However, having little choice, our DL called us into the showers – or ablutions, as they were now to be known – dressed only in our towels and crippling flip-flops, holding our wash bags – now known as dhobi bags. Clad only in a green issue towel, the DL stood confidently by the sinks and gave an introductory lesson in shaving that, for me, was quite informative. I'd shaved my pathetic excuse for a moustache when necessary (around once a month), but I'd only used my stepdad's electric shaver. I had never actually used a razor, something the DL picked up on straight away.

'Everyone here will shave every morning,' he said. 'Some of you hairy beasts may have to do it twice a day. Although I doubt that will be a problem for you... what's your name again?'

'Time, Corporal.'

'Ah, that's right, the pikey. Have you ever shaved properly, Time?'

'Not really, Corporal.'

'Not really? What does that mean? It's either yes or no.'

'No, Corporal.'

'Thought not. Can't afford a razor?'

I returned his smile, along with the giggles from the group. I was at least glad to be noticed.

'The first thing you need to know as a Royal Marine is that

when we shave, we always do it topless,' said the DL. 'I don't give a flying fuck if you've been shaving all your life with your top on – it stops now. It doesn't matter if it's minus forty, we take off our tops when we shave. If *ever* catch *anyone* shaving with a shirt or jumper or even a vest on, you can standby. Do we understand?'

The communal 'Yes, Corporal!' suggested we did.

After he finished, he called me up to show him I'd understood his demonstration. Standing next to him I felt rather childlike; his arms had more girth than my legs, his chest had hair. While not the most difficult task, I still managed to get it wrong, necessitating his shaving me. Rather than cutting my head off, as I feared he might, he was genuinely gentle and shaved me to perfection on one side before allowing me to finish off the other.

He then sent me back to the line and addressed the group again. 'Right, men, don't get excited,' he said. 'I'm going to get naked. If there are any beefers amongst you, hold back. You can have a wank after I've finished.'

I laughed along with the rest, though I had no idea what a beefer was. With that, the towel was gone. I don't think it was the first time he'd stripped naked in front of fifty men, as his confidence was startling in spite of him having a cocktail sausage for a cock. He then guided us through the importance of washing properly, demonstrating correct procedure in the shower. Reaching under his balls, he pulled out a large globule of what looked like shit that sat at the end of his finger.

'See,' he said. 'If we don't shower properly we might miss bits. If shit stays there it will cause infection.'

With that, he looked more closely at his finger before putting it into his mouth and sucking off whatever was stuck on the end, much to our disgust.

'Hmm,' he said, with a grin, 'I can't remember eating onions.'

\* \* \*

The first two weeks of commando training are known as induction. I loved it. No parents and I was allowed to stay up as long as I wanted. In fact, it was actively encouraged. How two washing machines, five irons and four ironing boards would suffice for fifty-two recruits to get their kit immaculately prepared before an early bedtime was anyone's guess. Ironing starch, boot polish, Brasso, and white blanco paste were my weapons of choice in those fledging weeks, and within the first few days I could polish a tap better than any sixteen-year-old I knew.

As the youngest of the intake I was at the bottom of the social order, one of the runts of the induction litter. We were the last to claim any piece of equipment or machinery to expedite the evening's administration, and we soon learnt the meaning of 'twos up' as a form of verbal queuing; 'twos up' would be followed by 'threes up', 'fours up', *et cetera*. I was often about 'forty-sixth up' for anything of use. But I consoled myself with the thought that, while my loser civvy mates back home would be in bed at 3am, I was enjoying ironing my crease-prone clothing through bleary eyes, trying to avoid the dangers of Irish pennants (those tiny threads that protrude from new clothing) and tram lines (unintended creases caused by careless ironing).

Cocooned within the induction block, fifty-two beds sat smartly in a row behind cloned lockers, our nice new shirts, boots and field equipment laid out exactly the same, our clothing folded to the size of the Royal Marines magazine, the famous *Globe & Laurel*.

On the third day, we had our first locker inspection. We stood to attention while the DL strode around with a menacing glint in his eye. Already there were several empty lockers, the legacy of guys who had already dropped out. Apparently, the Royal Marines wasn't for them – though how they could know that after just cleaning stuff I don't know. My pity for them extended only so far as to try and scrounge the washing powder they no longer needed.

I stood with my head as immobile as that of the recruit opposite, whom I knew only as Hopkins. At this early stage, we were still addressing each other formally by our surnames; nicknames were yet to be developed (mine would have been Dracula, as I was usually up all night).

The DL certainly didn't rush, taking an age to inspect the first few guys. Out of the corner of my eye, I could see lads flinching as their clothes were strewn over the floor in front of them.

After an hour or so of flying clothes and the DL's enlightening use of swear words, I realised that my feet ached. I hadn't stood still for so long since I'd won a musical statues contest at a school Christmas disco. On this occasion, I doubted I was going to win a stocking-shaped chocolate selection box. To my left, the DL was working himself into a nice lather.

'What in the name of fuckety-fuck is going on here?'

It was one of those questions impossible to answer. To do so could only dig an even deeper hole. Sensibly, the recruit, a bigger and much older lad than me, stood silent.

'Name?'

He was on safer ground with that one. 'Elliott, Corporal.'

'Do you know better than me, Elliott?

'No, Corporal.'

'Then why have you laid your locker out differently to how I told you?'

Another one that just couldn't be answered. Elliott remained schtum.

'You...'

A jumper flew through the air.

'...can...'

A shirt followed it.

'...stand...'

Elliott's water bottle hurtled past my face.

'...by!'

His webbing was kicked across the floor with an action that suggested the DL wasn't in the Corps football team. He closed in to eyeball Elliot, who arched backwards. With his body off balance, the DL pushed him with his index finger – not violently, just enough for Elliott to fall back. Catching his heel on the foot of the locker, he fully lost his balance and disappeared inside. The locker swayed to and fro with Elliot trying to steady himself, but only increasing the momentum. Hopkins found it funny, as did I. Not just funny – hilarious. Vastly against our better judgement, we started giggling.

To be fair, we tried to suppress it, but everyone knows that when you try to stop laughing all it does is hold the laughter cells in a queuing system in your throat where they call their mates along for a go. We tried to stop – oh, how we tried. I watched Hopkins turn a deep red, tears streaming from his eyes. I could see something had to give, and it was his nose. Within seconds it was bubbling with snot. I realised, to my horror, that I looked exactly the same.

Elliott's locker fell like a tree backwards, with the guy fighting all the way to keep himself upright. Green streams of snot were cascading volcanically down either side of Hopkins' philtrum. He was desperately sucking the slime into his mouth to hide the silent giggling but his teary eyes were a dead give-away, swivelling left and right like an eagle-eye Action Man (which I'd longed for but never received) from the DL to me to the locker-clad Elliott, frantically trying to scramble free from his chipboard tomb.

Like a shiny-booted obscenity tornado, the DL laid waste to anyone and everyone's locker. Seemingly bored of shouting, when he approached mine he simply stared at my snot-covered face and threw out all my belongings without so much as a courteous introduction.

Around the induction block, when the shiny floors weren't covered in recruits' clothing, everything was immaculate and ordered – a not-so-subtle hint for us to achieve the same. The walls were perfectly lined with pictures of Royal Marines participating in feats of derring-do, and Corps history posters; all well before the corporate world got hold of smug motivational posters with words like 'teamwork' below a picture of ants lifting a leaf or some other shite. These posters were there to invoke the *esprit de corps*, the primal glue that bonds together the men of the Royal Marines.

With us all packed tightly together, we got to know our comrades quicker. We were making the first steps toward camaraderie. This togetherness was underpinned by lectures about the history and traditions of the Royal Marines. The importance of these lessons could not be underestimated. We needed to know what we aspired to be part of and where we stood in the grand scheme of things.

Learning a new language was also included in splinter lessons. Although sat apart like a dog in a cattery, Royal Marines are officially part of the Royal Navy, so we learned 'jackspeak' slang to embed us further into our new culture. Those lucky few who made it through the course would be known as plain 'royals', or, more commonly, 'bootnecks' – so called for the leather neck collars worn in days of old by our forebears to prevent mutinous sailors from slitting their throats whilst on guard duty. One assumes this led to a rise in stab wounds to the chest.

As mere recruits we were nicknamed 'nods', perhaps due to our persistent nodding off from being awake twenty hours a day. Sailors were 'matelots'. Army personnel were called 'pongos', because their questionable hygiene levels gave rise to the old military phrase, 'where the army goes, the pong goes'. The RAF, the most civilian of the forces, were known as 'crabfats' due to their uniform being exactly the same colour as the lotion used by military personnel to get rid of pubic lice. It's amazing what you could learn even before the advent of the internet.

We were under the command of 'Pusser', the slang word for 'the service'. Everything would have the prefix 'Pusser', so a service-issue suitcase would become a 'Pusser's grip'. Anyone who was 100 per cent service through and through would be known as 'Pusser's'.

I never did find out who Harry was, but he was talked about often. Any adjective could have the prefix 'Harry' added to it, and be suffixed with '-ers', '-bats', or '-pigs'. For example: to expand on the word 'wazz' being slang for 'good', we could say 'Harry Wazzbats'. To be cold: 'Harry Icepigs'. Without money: 'Harry Skinters'. Ronnie was Harry's brother, so if Harry was being overworked we could use him instead, e.g. hot: 'Ronnie Redpigs'.

The toilets were now 'heads', and steak and kidney puddings 'babies' heads'. Conversely, our actual heads became 'grids', 'nappers' or 'fat ones'.

Jackspeak convention decrees that anyone with the surname 'Smith' will be rechristened 'Smudge', a 'Brown' will become 'Buster', a 'Bell' will be 'Dinger'. Anyone who shared a famous surname would have their real first name destroyed forever and replaced with their famous counterpart's. Dave Forsyth, for instance, would be known forevermore as 'Bruce'. There are men who I was extremely close to, yet I never knew their real first names. Some surnames, such as 'Driver', could have a myriad of new first names attached such as 'Screwy', or even, 'This par-four is short enough for me to use a two-iron rather than my', although, in truth, I rarely heard the last one.

We also learnt how to talk in abbreviations and acronyms:

SLR – Self-Loading Rifle.

GPMG – General Purpose Machine Gun.

CEMO – Combat Equipment Marching Order.

LCU – Landing Craft Utility.

MUPPET – Most Useless Person Pusser Ever Trained.

So, despite not even being in a dogwatch, within two shakes of a donkey's flip-flop we gobbed off in new tongues trying not to grip the shit of the pit monsters attempting to get their nappers down and bash out the zeds while we glopped goffers or NATO standard wets and scranning nutty while spinning hoofing dits about mega essence or rats' gronks and pashes we had trapped while Harry Mingbats as strawberry mivvies - gen.

Every waking minute was taken up with the militaristic ethos and incessant subliminal messages to condition us. It was like a religious experience, and we were rapidly being converted. Our DL was the military equivalent of the Rev Jim Jones. While I don't think he wanted to give us poisoned Kool-Aid, the Pusser's orange cordial came close.

I actually looked forward to our PT lessons, even though pre-workout nerves always forced me to evacuate my bowels first. On the PRC, we'd been put through the USMC physical test to gauge our fitness, and now we attempted as many press-ups and sit-ups we could muster in two minutes, and how many pull-ups we could max out on. Having the body weight of a malnourished puppy, my achievements were better than average – although on the 200m shuttle sprint, my short legs left me some way behind the quicker lads.

Finishing off, we trotted out of the camp to do a basic fitness test run: a one-and-a-half mile troop run/walk to be completed in fifteen minutes, which to all intents and purposes was a warm-up to the return run, where we would race the same distance back to camp as individuals. Although we had eleven-and-a-half minutes to complete it, if we'd taken that long on our PRC we wouldn't have made it there.

I was near the back, completing it in eight minutes thirty seconds, over two minutes behind the racing snakes at the front. My time was similar to that on my PRC, but then I'd completed it in comfortable footwear. Here I ran in those cardboard-thin daps, over tarmac and asphalt, where treading on anything resembling a pebble would throw you off balance in pain. Just to check we weren't loafing, we then did it all again for good measure. No wonder many recruits suffered shin splints and stress fractures from running in those things. It was the only time as a Royal Marine we would ever do a BFT (battle fitness training) in trainers; thereafter, it would always be in those RMHCB boots designed by the Italian Mafia.

Physical training at this stage was known as IMF – initial military fitness. We dressed smartly in our pusser's daps, stretchy socks that I'd only previously seen on schoolgirls, and thick linen shorts that could only be sufficiently ironed at the same temperature as the earth's core. To complete our IMF kit, we had a choice of either green or white rugby-type shirt. When I first looked at myself in the mirror in this get-up, it made me look less like a commando than an extra in some Ealing comedy about a public-school sports day.

IMF was about as far removed from expected physical training as one could imagine. The gym floor, I only now noticed, was a huge game of dot to dot where each of us would stand over our designated spot then, upon command, walk around the gym, first in a sort of stiff marching motion then with one leg tensed to slam into the floor, making us all look like we wore calipers.

Upon returning to our spots, the PTI stood proud on his dais before demonstrating arm movements to improve our coordination in the style of a tic-tac man at the races. It was beyond me how this was going to make me a commando, but it seemed that this warm-up was just a distraction from the real exercise. Around the walls stood those wooden beams that in school we called 'apparatus'. They would be the framework upon which we would conduct countless sit-ups, press-ups and pull-ups, both in time to the PTI's numbered calls and in our own time, where we would push out the designated number in the quickest possible time: a quick fifty here, a slow fifty there, over and over again until every sinew of muscle had been stretched, pulled and tweaked until it screamed for mercy.

Finally, my favourite, the rope climbing, would see us scale the 30ft ropes using a highly-efficient climbing method where the legs did the majority of the work, thankfully making my weedy grip of only minimal importance. We would wrap ourselves around the ropes halfway back down to make safe and then invert ourselves so we descended upside down. As I hung like a bat from the rope I smiled, knowing this was the stuff I wanted to be doing, the first time I'd done anything I considered commando-like. One thing I didn't want to do was follow the examples of some lads who found the rope climbing overly difficult, one falling head first down to a sickening crash on the hard floor.

'I said controlled descent, Lofty,' shouted the primary PTI in the direction of the whimpering, snotty heap at the foot of the rope. 'Once you've stopped making strange noises, we'll think about getting you some help.'

'Don't bleed on my floor,' added a secondary.

For some reason the nod, bleeding from a head wound, didn't see the funny side; probably not least because the bloodstain was going to make washing his IMF top a whole lot harder.

# FOUR

*'When we are tired, we are attacked by those ideas we conquered long ago.'*
FRIEDRICH NIETZSCHE, PHILOSOPHER

MUCH TO MY disappointment, we did very little of anything that resembled soldiering while in induction.

We wouldn't even get our hands on a weapon until week three. But in those first two weeks I learnt how to march quite smartly in pseudo-unison with fifty or so others, feeling proud that I could complete complex tasks such as putting one leg in front of the other, turning and stopping.

On a drill square, even walking properly is difficult. Military marching is a mental balancing act of walking at a 30" pace, crashing your heels firmly into the tarmac parade ground and swinging your arms level with the shoulders, elbows locked, thumbs pressed hard on top of fists, head immobile on your shoulders – unless we were trying out the complex new move of saluting to the left/right, all in time to the howling sarcasm of the DL. According to him, when anyone marched slightly wrongly a village was deprived of its idiot, or Joey Deacon was missing his less able brother.

Prior to getting mobilised, the drill square was the scene of many a tense inspection. The DL would slowly make his way along the front rank. Due to my height I'd been positioned in the middle of the second rank, so I had plenty of time to gauge his mood. Even if the recruit was immaculate he would suffer.

DL to recruit (who returns his look): 'Do you fancy me?'

'No, Corporal.'

'So you think I'm ugly then?'

'No, Corporal.'

'So you do fancy me then. Give me fifty for being a noshbag.'

So the previously immaculate recruit, was not only accused of lusting after the drill sergeant, but now irrevocably creased up by press-ups on the tarmac of the parade square.

Anything even slightly less than perfect was picked up on, especially if it was fluff on our 'wee beret'. The kind of thing a normal human could only see with the aid of an electron microscope stood out like a sore thumb to the DL.

'Do you know why it's called a wee beret, Lofty?' the DL would ask, the blue beret swinging on his finger.

'Because I have a small head, Corporal?'

'*Weeeee!*' the DL would shriek, throwing it twenty metres over the adjacent hedge.

The guardian of the drill square was the 'first drill'. The bastion of everything ceremonial in the Corps, he was a sternly anhedonic warrant officer whose presence made everyone extra nervous, despite his head looking like a suet pudding. His voice had all the tenderness of an air-raid klaxon, and his beady eye was cast not only us but also the instruction of our DL. Only years later would we find out that the DL we looked up to as one step up from God wasn't overly respected by his peers, and was actually known as the 'last drill'.

At the time, some bright spark at the MOD (there's a lot of them, apparently) decided to reintroduce puttees for a trial period. Puttees are hessian wraps designed to protect the ankle as a buffer between the bottom of battle fatigues and boots. They were so old fashioned that they were introduced around the time the Dead Sea first went sick, and taken from service not long after. We wore them with our denims, but only for drill in our initiation weeks. Our DL had somehow forgotten to tell us how to put them on correctly, possibly due to not really knowing; after all, they had been discontinued way before even his time.

I ended up just wrapping them around in an 'I've broken my leg' sort of way, gaining a B grade in first-aid bandage. It left me looking like a cross between a Japanese sniper and a 1950s golfer. Take a few steps and they would unravel, leaving me looking like the Andrex puppy.

On parade, a marine turns up wearing only one.

Inspecting officer: 'Why are you only wearing one puttee?'

Marine: 'I could only find one, sir.'

Inspecting officer: 'Well, don't you think it would look better with no puttees?'

Marine: 'Yes sir, I do.'

Inspecting officer: 'Well, sort it out, then.'

The marine bends down to untie his puttee, unwrapping the yards of cloth. As the last of the puttee comes away he finds his other one underneath wrapped around the same ankle...

As a sixteen-year-old I was chuffed when I got picked up on a drill inspection for not shaving correctly. However, pride in my newfound manliness was slightly dampened when I had to run back to the accommodation to fetch shaving kit and a mess tin full of cold water to re-shave at the side of the drill square, while fellow recruits ran around the square for misdemeanours such as dull boots, dirty brasses or having uneven ears.

Still to this day I wonder at the relevance of those many hours on the drill square. Sure, we needed to know how to march and salute. Discipline, order and team building were integral, but the military ethos and fieldwork can facilitate those mechanics. The historical importance of drill cannot be ignored, but in today's theatre of war it pales into total insignificance. Maybe we just like to do it for traditional purposes, Pavlov's dogs performing to the crowds at Buckingham Palace. But as a teenager in my first few weeks of training, I continued unabated in my quest to complicate something as easy as walking.

\* \* \*

Our first venture out of CTC was Exercise First Step. It could hardly be regarded as a commando operation; it was more like a camping trip to instill in us the basics of building a low-lying tactical shelter known as a bivvy, and how to cook our rations.

Again, washing was an inherent part of these field lectures – this time conducted by two corporals to whom we'd been briefly introduced when taking our oath. A bivvy poncho separated the pair. The corporal at the front had his arms hidden, replaced by the arms of the corporal behind. Watching the rear man operating blind, undressing the corporal at the front, was hilarious, especially when shaving. The shaving brush swathed foam all over the face of the first corporal, and then his nose and cheeks. It was evident that not only did the corporals have a sense of self-effacing humour, there was trust between the two – especially when the rear guy cleaned under his mate's foreskin and removed shavings of processed cheese, which he then placed in his mouth.

I was bivvied up with Hopkins. Our friendship blossomed after Elliott had been swallowed by his locker, and we'd built up a bit of a bond. Hopkins was the total opposite of me. He had lived in Germany, Hong Kong and Gibraltar; I'd been to Ibiza once on a package holiday. My real father was a mysterious Spaniard in the UK on a building project, who seemingly liked impregnating young waitresses but not the responsibility of sticking around. His father was a respected lieutenant colonel in the British Army, who had sent Hopkins to boarding school from the age of eight. He'd learned to look after himself from an early age and, while not academically outstanding, had passed his 'A' levels. He was a good-looking bastard as well, and his physical prowess was pretty impressive. He had the body of an Olympic gymnast, and already seemed to find the gym sessions slightly less arduous than most of us.

There was one small problem. He didn't want to be there. The youngest of four brothers, the others had all joined the army as officers and, as per family tradition, he was expected to follow suit. So he decided to join the Corps, not as an officer but as a ground-level marine, just to buck the trend. While his father was happy that he'd at least joined the military, Hopkins had only done it out of family duty. It was going to be a long thirty weeks for him.

But he had a coolness born from having done this sort of thing for the last ten years and, as a mandatory member of his school's cadet force, Exercise First Step was just another weekend for him, unlike me who'd only spent nights out under canvas in holiday parks with drunken aunts and uncles. It was like having a personal tutor, and the ease with which he took to all the field tasks made me think he'd be promoted not long after training. It was he, not the training team, who really showed me how to put up a bivvy, and it was he who showed me the delights of a twenty-four-hour ration pack.

Single-man 'ratpacks' were issued to troops with little logistical back-up, and as commandos we came under this definition. They came in four menus, mouthwateringly named A, B, C and D, and as an eight-man group we were given two of each to try.

Menu C was steak and kidney pudding, which contained mostly lumps of fat and gristle, and kidneys that tasted like they'd been on dialysis for a few months. Menu A – chicken curry – was my favourite. However, it was best eaten during the day: when the tin was opened our bodies would light up in the reflection of the day-glo orange gloop. If opened under the cover of darkness it would instantly give away our position.

Other tins contained either a bacon burger or a bacon grill. Giving them different names was an obvious ploy to make us think we were getting variety. None of it mattered much, anyway. After Exercise First Step we were only ever issued menu B but given two choices – eat it or starve.

The ubiquitous confectionary pack consisted of Arabic 'Rolos' that even in the heat of the summer broke teeth, or even worse, a packet of out-of-date Spangles. In the civilian world these actually tickled the palate; when given the military makeover, the wrapper was fused to the sweets and it was physically impossible to unwrap them. During any given night in the field, you'd hear the constant spitting of plastic from guys sucking wrapped Spangles on sentry.

As a biscuit connoisseur, 'Biscuits Brown' and 'Biscuits Fruit AB' were a great disappointment. Both retained the consistency of low-grade cardboard; the fruit AB was just a poor imitation of the world-famous garibaldi. If the Italian revolutionary had offered the military version to his republican troops they'd have hung him in mutiny.

Finally, there was a sundries pack containing bitter coffee granules that would stick to Teflon, teabags so bad they were only used as the filling for homemade cigarettes, and a book of matches that struggled to light oxygen on a still day. If the wind rose above 0.5 on the Beaufort scale, we'd have to resort to windproof matches that were great if you could light things within a micro-second. To complete this plastic bag of useful items there was John Wayne toilet paper – so called because it took shit from no one.

To add finesse to this delectable culinary experience, we always cooked on the woodland floor which was covered in a carpet of pine needles. These would stick to any moist surface, and made it almost impossible to eat or drink anything without a side serving of the spiky little bastards. Everything we ate became infused with the taste of pine needles and like anything sharp, they weren't particularly pleasant to swallow.

Watching guys cook was probably akin to commando *Masterchef*. I say 'probably' because I never watched anyone – I was too busy cooking in my own personal hell to bother about anyone else. It wouldn't have been so bad if we'd had all day to cook everything up on a four-ring gas hob. Unfortunately, even on a leisurely day, we had about fifteen minutes with a small, bear trap-like stove that used hexamine blocks as fuel. These blocks gave off fumes that could kill a horse, though luckily they didn't burn for very long – certainly not long enough to properly cook food, but enough to heat the metal stove to a temperature that took the skin from your hands in the mad rush to clear up after eating.

Invariably, I would end up stuffing half my rations back into my large pack, leaving even less room for the next lot. Often, we ate our rations cold to save time. In the summer this wasn't a problem, but as training progressed through the colder months, hot food would become an emotional, as well as physical, spur.

Of course, after the speed eating and drinking that left

indigestion burbling away within our sweaty bodies, every culinary accessory had to be spotlessly clean. If even a grain of salt was noted on the KFS fork on field inspection, then food poisoning would be a welcome alternative to the punishment we'd receive. If the merest speck of black should be found on a mess tin, pain followed. Unfortunately, whether by accident or perverse design, hexamine blocks leave a sticky black residue on the base of a mess tin slightly harder to remove than caramelised soot mixed with woodchip wallpaper. It wasn't too bad if you got to it while still damp, but if you let it dry it was like removing week-old Weetabix from a bowl.

Despite all of this, eating rations and assembling a bivvy was quite exhilarating for me. I thought myself a tad nearer to being a commando as I'd used my webbing as a pillow and, although non-tactical, spent most of the night with one eye open, waiting to batter to death any approaching enemy with my new weapon: a mini-baton made from the packet of Arabic Rolos.

Other than the four-mile run back to camp wearing new boots that started to slice up my feet from the ninth pace, Exercise First Step was the easiest thing I'd yet done, mainly due to Hopkins. But for him, just being there must have been extremely difficult.

Back at CTC I did a lot more physical exercise: more walking in circles in various well-pressed, if ill-fitting, uniforms; saluting; trying to remember my new first name; cleaning everything from the cheese under my foreskin to the soles of my boots to the inside of a toilet. More than once, I reflected that if I failed Royal Marines training I'd be able to start my own cleaning empire and call it something ridiculous like the Gleam Team.

What I didn't do much of was sleep. On nights when I did manage to get to bed before 03.00, the DL would invariably come in and wake us with some important task like reciting Royal Marines Victorian Cross winners, or chanting the weight of a 7.62mm self-loading rifle.

One night, he came in offering a nighttime snack. 'Anyone like a teacake?' he said, cheerfully.

Elliott, keen to redeem himself after the locker incident, bravely accepted his offer. Depending on where you come from in the UK, a teacake is a current bun, a bread roll or a scone-like pastry. I don't know anywhere other than CTC where a teacake would be a large lump of butter atop a dry teabag. Elliott ate it. It was better than many of the disgusting items that would pass my lips in the years to come.

Whatever reason we were awoken for, I found the tone of our wake-up calls humorous, never feeling threatened or bullied by the DL's antics. Looking back, it was to test our resolve as sleep deprivation is the catalyst for many a person to quit in any walk of life. There would be many more sleep-deprived weeks to come.

We were also deprived of time. Although induction was meant to prepare us for the rigours of training, it was a full-on, twenty-four-hour carousel of running around, cleaning, lectures and physical exertion. We were often late and the DL, after a generous allocation of very slow press-ups, explained we needed to 'make time'. What a classic!

General relativity allows for the existence of 'closed time-like curves' and, in theory, time travel into the past. The first equations that permitted closed time curves were proposed by Kurt Gödel in 1949 – a solution known as the 'Gödel metric'. We had to solve the elusive 'nod metric' that would have allowed a Royal Marines recruit to deal with the seemingly insoluble issues posed by these curvatures in space-time. Unfortunately, I never did solve it and I never knew anyone who did. (I did know a few bootnecks with a GCSE in woodwork, though.) So we joined the most revered physicians in history in being unable to 'make time' within a stand easy. Einstein, however, was never thrashed for being adrift.

I was the only one still awake. Trying as best I could to fold down the ironing board without wrestling it to the ground, I looked at the clock. It was 02.05. It was the earliest I had yet managed to finish. The outer door opened and in strode a corporal with all the purpose of a man carrying a toilet roll to the loo. I stood to attention immediately, holding my ironing board reverently upright.

'Stand by your beds!' he yelled, switching on the lights in the darkened room. 'Stand by your beds!'

I ran to my locker and stood again to attention. It was the first time since starting training that I'd been the first to do anything. I didn't feel quite so tired now either, as the adrenalin pumped through my veins.

The rest of the troop, bleary-eyed and half-naked, did their best to stand to attention, some with a morning glory showing within their boxers. The strange corporal walked down the middle of the room with his hands behind his back. He looked a bit like a physics teacher, only more menacing and without elbow patches. He regarded an indeterminate point somewhere in the far distance.

'I have been hearing things about you lot,' he said. His tone suggested otherwise. 'And it has not impressed me.

*I was right about some things.*

'It seems you have difficulty grasping the concept of getting ready on time. You lot think you can turn up when you want and not give a fuck. Well, let me tell you fellas, *I* give a fuck. In the Falklands, we lost men 'cos people like you were adrift.'

I didn't really know where he was going with this. I did suspect that, whatever the outcome, it wouldn't be what I wanted at this unearthly hour.

'Five minutes, outside Portsmouth Company HQ building in gash PT rig. Go.'

He walked out of the induction block, leaving a bevy of nods climbing into their lockers to take out their civilian PT kit. I only needed to don my trainers, so ran as fast as my legs would carry me to the meeting place where the corporal stood, hands on hips like a superhero, his body silhouetted against the light behind. He said nothing as we arrived in dribs and drabs, only occasionally looking at his watch. We stood in three ranks, hanging on his every word like dogs awaiting a Barbara Woodhouse command.

'Five minutes, I said,' he intoned, his voice calm and level. He sounded like he was going to read us a bedtime story. 'It has taken you six. You lot are taking the piss. When I say "go" you lazy twats will run as fast as you can, up past the guardroom, back down the main drag and meet me by the water tank.'

Even though we were stood at ease we were as primed as anyone could be at such an unearthly hour, as if the corporal was Ron Pickering at the start of a *We Are the Champions* race.

'Stand by, go.'

With only a survival instinct to guide us, we hurtled up towards the guardroom and back down the camp to the bottom field. The individual speed of nods differed and the troop was soon strung out, leaving the slower ones a couple of hundred metres behind the racing snakes. No one even thought of making use of the many short cuts we passed. We daren't.

I reached the water tank with my breath rasping. The corporal stood there as before: silently, menacingly, and, as it turned out, impatiently.

'Everyone here?' Again his voice was cool and quiet. 'Good. Front support position place.'

We automatically spread out and adopted the press-up position. We held the position, until our stomachs started to cramp.

'Arms bend.'

We bent our arms and they remained in place, shaking under tension.

'Six minutes to get ready.' He walked around slowly. 'Six long minutes.'

The gurgling of those struggling to hold the press-up position punctured the cool night air.

'Why it took so long I don't know. Arms stretch.'

We straightened our arms, relieving the tension in our

triceps and shoulders only for the pain to transfer to our stomachs and groin. His silence was deafening.

'Even after that warning, it seems only a few of you put the effort in to get here in good time. It has taken you lot another four-and-a-half minutes to get here. Not good enough, men. Arms bend.'

His soothing tones didn't make the deathly slow press-ups any easier.

'It shows me some of you are loafing...'

One nod's body weight collapsed, as he could hold the position no longer.

The corporal didn't shout, just made a quiet threat that reminded me of an evil Bond villain. 'Get your chest off the fucking ground.'

He carried on after the rude interruption.

'...Yes, loafing. And you're not even out of induction yet. Stretch.'

The gasps of relief rolled around the prostrate group as we locked our arms straight again.

'You have wasted ten-and-a-half minutes of my life, so I am wasting ten-and-a-half minutes of yours. Arms bend.'

The agonised groans told me many were struggling to hold the position. I was one of them. Twisting the arms against the body relieved the shoulders, only to isolate the triceps, a different yet equally substantial pain that made the teeth grit rather than the face gurn. When held in this position for such a long time it becomes rather undignified. Dribbling is the norm, snot bubbles burst from the nose as breathing becomes difficult and eyes are squeezed so tightly that stars appear (with no Mathew Kelly in sight). It was a long ten-and-a-half minutes of agonising press-ups; it was a good job we'd only done about 200 in our earlier PT session.

'Stretch. Right, stand up.'

We struggled to our feet, the lactic acid burning our quivering arms. I looked around the darkened faces; few seemed particularly overjoyed.

'When I say go, you are to run, jump in the tank and be back here within thirty seconds. Go.'

It wasn't too difficult to meet his strict deadline. The silent, shimmering water tank was only ten metres away, and the piercing cold water only encouraged the most fleeting of dunkings. We returned to our press-up area, the sound of dripping clothing drumming the hard-mudded area beneath our feet.

'You lot have not impressed me one bit. I don't know who I've upset, but I am going to be with you for the next twenty-eight weeks. You better start switching on, or I will start switching some of you fuckers off.'

I hoped that was it. My body was starting to cool and the cold, wet clothing was causing goose bumps to ripple my skin. At least we could go back to the accommodation now.

'Front support position place. Arms bend.'

I was wrong. Apparently, we had only completed six minutes of press-ups. We carried on again for an extra four-and-a-half minutes, completing two extremely slow and difficult press-ups in our soaking wet clothes.

The novelty of staying up late was beginning to wear off. We tramped back to the induction block, and the general consensus amongst the drenched group was that this corporal was there just to fuck us about and welcome us as induction recruits. Never mind, induction would finish in a few days and we could maybe get a bit more sleep after this.

How ridiculously naïve were we?

\* \* \*

The two-week induction phase completed, our DL introduced us to the rest of the training team who would now become the most important men in our lives. One of them was the corporal who had beasted us on the bottom field at silly o'clock the week before. He said little and smiled even less, so we named him 'the Unsmiling Assassin'.

We were evenly split into sections of ten men, which was easy as only forty of us remained, and were now to be led by a section corporal. Just below God in importance, the section corporal would assess the amount of punishment we would receive, while giving the appropriate amount of instruction to facilitate our progress. Above him was the troop sergeant who, in our case, was an aged alcoholic. Supposedly above them all was the troop officer who, in reality, was just there to do administration and talk posh.

Luckily, I wasn't thrown into the Unsmiling Assassin's section; our section was headed by Corporal Stevens. A good-looking, chisel-jawed Adonis, he wore the 'King's Badge', meaning he had been the best recruit when in training. He was also a sniper. All in all, I was in total awe of him. Here was a man who had been chosen to shape us into future commandos, our mentor, guide and disciplinarian; a man of integrity and honour who would instill these commendable traits through careful guidance, education, and prolonged bouts of intense pain.

Leaving the induction block as immaculate as we'd found it for the next troop of new joiners, our new accommodation was in one of the ghastly white behemoths that towered over the rest of the camp. The view across the River Exe from my room was worth a million dollars. The estuary flow had receded, leaving a dark-brown mud flat. Adjacent to the train platform, the mud had been temporarily tattooed with footmarks spelling '519 Troop'. With a recruit troop every two weeks, it seemed that these guys in week ten had severely fucked up and been offered a mud run in lieu of death by firing squad.

Although the view was splendid, I never had much time to relax and appreciate it. I was endlessly running from one lecture to another, repeatedly changing uniform like a catwalk model, just without the long legs. It was information overload into a brain buzzing twenty hours a day.

My mates in the sixth form at school would be getting up at 8am to dress slovenly, in an un-pressed school uniform. I was now up at 05.30 to undertake industrial-standard cleaning, before ramming down my full-fat breakfast ahead of a 07.30 morning accommodation and uniform inspection, or a run, or whatever surprise the training team had up their smartly-rolled sleeves. This ranged from a locker inspection to snap shower inspection – only to find one of the training team having a shower, which would lead to us being punished for not having the showers ready for inspection.

Making my bed now took longer than the whole of my pre-school routine. In these times of duvets it seems hard to fathom that making a bed could take ten minutes or more, but the carefully-ironed bed sheets and blankets had to be folded down neatly and tightly at the top. On Wednesdays, it all had to be folded at both top and bottom, presumably to show we hadn't slept in our boots. On other days we would have to make a bed pack, a specially-designed wrapping where sheets, blankets and pillow had to be measured, folded and wrapped inside the cover sheet to look like a giant Mr Kipling cake. This was for no other reason than to ensure we had to strip and remake our beds – and to remind us of Mr Kipling cakes.

Whichever bed design we had to create, once made it was treated like a house of cards – impossible to go near for fear of wrecking. So immaculate did we make them, all that was missing was a ribbon with a 'Happy Mother's Day' card attached. It was not at all unknown, prior to more formal room inspections, for lads to make their beds to perfection the night before and then sleep on the cold linoleum floor. Six hours of discomfort was far more appealing than another series of punishment exercises for having a slightly creased sheet. It was easy to work out whether the bed was made to an acceptable standard. If it was, it would remain intact. If it was not, it would be thrown around the room, and sometimes out of the window, to the accompaniment of loud expletives, before being trodden on by the corporal's polished boot – necessitating yet more washing, drying and ironing.

# FIVE

*'If there's one thing this last week has taught me, it's better to have a gun and not need it than to need a gun and not have it.'*

CLARENCE WORLEY, *TRUE ROMANCE*

WHEN EVENTUALLY ISSUED a weapon, I found I wasn't very good with it. Being a nervous recruit with a vast two weeks of experience, the drills barked by Corporal Stevens, although clear and succinct, just went in one ear and out the other. It didn't help that most of the guys in my section had been in the cadets, or were mechanics or safebreakers in their previous lives. They all had far more practical ability than me, my childlike dexterity accentuating my slowness.

Hopkins soon became Corporal Stevens' favourite. Not only because he allowed the corporal's sheepdog to shag his leg when ordered to 'act like a Wren' (a female sailor), but because he was good at everything. While I fumbled nervously with my gas plug, forgot to tap my pouches or panicked over some complex instruction such as 'load', Hopkins would understand first time, every time, and then demonstrate his competency with seemingly consummate ease. To boot, his suave looks complemented his friendly persona, making him an all-round 'double yolker' of a man. It was sickening really.

Theoretical instruction was easier to 'inwardly digest'. I could remember the parts of the weapon perfectly, and so too the contents of the cleaning wallet: combination tool, oil container, wire brush, cleaning brush, cleaning rod, pull through and flannelette. Not everyone was blessed with so retentive a memory. During one such session, Corporal Stevens asked a recruit the contents of the wallet. He held up a cleaning rod. 'What's this then, Lofty?'

'Uh, I don't know, Corporal,' the recruit replied. You could almost smell the terror.

Corporal Stevens looked exasperated. 'Right,' he said. 'I'll give you a clue. It is a cleaning *blank*.'

The recruit still looked confused, as Corporal Stevens tried to extract the word 'rod' from his sponge-like brain.

'Uh…' This was going to be a long lesson.

'Okay…' said Corporal Stevens. 'Think of the first name of a famous person whose surname is "Stewart", and then add it to the end of "cleaning".'

A forty-watt bulb dimly lit up above the recruit's head, and a look of excitement crossed his face. 'I've got it, Corporal!'

'Excellent, so what is it? Cleaning…?'

'Jackie!' said the recruit.

My own imbecilic struggle with weapons drills meant I got fitter quicker, as my fuck-ups always resulted in a form of physical punishment commonly known as a beasting. Beastings were commonplace during recruit training. Indeed, rumour had it they were part of the syllabus, just never advertised. They were the equivalent of pensioner sex, or stepping in dog shit: you knew it was going to happen at some point, but you felt sick at the thought of it.

Known for their character-building properties, beastings were a form of tough love. The punishments involved strange yet resourceful exercises, with varying pain settings repeated until the recruits were totally exhausted. Often, the troop sergeant would end a bollocking with a phrase that forever struck terror into our hearts: 'You lot can stand by.'

The phrase still haunts me to this day. Even Tammy Wynette's 'Stand By Your Man' gives me the chills.

It was like being given the death sentence. We knew pain would come, the only variables being when and how much. The thought of impending doom would gnaw at the back of my mind until the event happened. From an outsider's perspective beastings may seem a form of abuse, but as a sixteen-year-old commando-in-waiting, while not overly excited about it, I was willing to get beasted every day if it meant getting a green beret.

This was life at Commando Training Centre: a consuming whirlwind of excess, shouting and running; a mind-boggling mechanical bucking bull that wanted to throw me off. All I could do was hold on just a little tighter in an ever more difficult attempt to keep on.

\* \* \*

Our first real venture as wannabe commandos was on Exercise Twosome, or 'Gruesome Twosome' as it was affectionately known. This was something so completely different from anything I'd ever experienced in my short life that, for the first time, I wondered whether joining the Royal Marines had been a wise move.

The previous troop that returned from Gruesome Twosome had recently made the newspapers after it was revealed one of their recruits had been fed a shit sandwich. We couldn't understand the problem: I certainly hadn't had a good one yet. Then we realised that it was literally a *shit* sandwich, and we understood why his mother had contacted the press.

Although the training teams were warned similar actions would not be tolerated by the anti-shit-eating mandarins of Whitehall, it little changed our team's intentions of making Gruesome Twosome live up to its reputation.

The exercise was an introduction into basic fieldwork, our bread and butter as potential commandos. One of our first lectures was on how to properly apply camouflage cream (cam cream). Split into pairs, I was hoping to partner up with Hopkins, but I was like the bespectacled kid with the wonky legs when being picked for a game of football. Everyone partnered off with someone they could trust, leaving me searching for a partner of equal incompetence.

The other guy standing alone was Jackie; I forget his real name, but he was so-called after his 'cleaning Jackie' fauxpas. He had struggled with every element of training so far. The only thing he seemed competent in was grumbling and he 'dripped' at every incidence of hardship, which, with the regime we were under, was quite often. We were all in it together so his constant whining had not made him at all popular. Neither, it seemed, was I. With no other options available, we begrudgingly paired up.

The first thing he said was, 'You know I'm leaving at the end of the week? This is all bollocks.'

*Oh, great.* Not only was my partner shit at fieldcraft, he had no interest in improving.

The lessons were based on the 'buddy buddy' system, where each recruit checks the other to ensure both are 'squared away' and suitably prepared for whatever lies ahead. We had to cam up our partners, the idea being that we would both practice the application but also learn to entrust ourselves to our buddy.

My buddy was about as friendly as Adolf Eichmann, and his coverage of my face was poor, to say the least. Of course, he got picked up when I was inspected; I blended into the background like a cow in a pigsty. To be fair, Jackie was given twice the amount of press-ups I was, which wasn't ideal for him as he could only do half the press-ups I could. These were made all the harder by Corporal Stevens shoving the cam cream bag nozzle up each nostril and filling them with the thick, brown gunk.

'Time?'

'Yes, Corporal?' I answered from the floor, sounding like Malcolm from the Vicks Sinex advert.

'Now you look like you've sneezed your own impacted bowel, you'd better scrub yourself clean and start again.'

I glared at Jackie. He was the twat that had got me into this predicament. It didn't have much of an effect though, he was too busy scooping acrid cam cream from his mouth whilst enduring some rather vulgar language from Corporal Stevens.

'When I come back you'd both better be as clean as Princess Diana's knickers or you can stand by.'

Without the aid of plentiful, hot, running water – or indeed, any water at all – this was going to be a hard task. We had been issued with the one water bottle per day with which we were also supposed to cook, wash ourselves and our cooking implements, and fight off dehydration. Luckily, the exercise was held in the hottest August since 1976 so drinking was clearly optional

It was around now when I reflected that getting camouflaged seemed somehow less appealing than it appeared in the recruit-ment brochures. They certainly hadn't shown the discomfort of sweating like a cheap beef salad while lying awkwardly in spiky gorse bushes, with twigs, leaves and broken branches scraping, cutting and scoring the skin leaving me feeling like I had been buggered by a sexually frustrated Laburnum.

In between being jabbed, poked, kicked and thrashed around the local vicinity, we had further theoretical instruction in the large marquee that doubled as the training team's accommodation and lecture room. Any notification was usually in the form of, 'Right, you fuckers, you were told to be ready for your next session, and by the look of it you have been swanning/arsing about/loafing/ignoring us/taking the piss [delete as required]. You have got five minutes to get your shit together and be in the marquee for a lecture on...'

On this occasion it was 'sentry duty'. I consoled myself with the thought that at least the lesson on the duties of a sentry *had* to be easy. I based this forlorn hope on my extensive research of sentry duty that mainly involved watching lots of old war films. It seemed to entail a lot of walking up and down a designated path, usually in the opposite direction to any silent enemy, while sharing cigarettes, and talking German.

Unfortunately the reality of a sentry duty lecture was a lot different.

'When you are a sentry, fellas, you are the eyes and ears of the troop,' said the Unsmiling Assassin looking rather sinister behind his lectern. 'So it is vitally important you are awake, alert and aware of your surroundings. Falling asleep is the biggest no-no of all when on sentry and you not only show a lack of discipline, you show true selfishness putting your own needs before your oppos. This scant regard for the team ethic lets not only your mates down, but also puts them in grave danger. You are the early warning system and it is up to you to alert your troop of any possible enemy approach.'

In the steam of a humid tent, in the early afternoon heat, immediately after lunch, trying to stay awake and alert while learning *how to* stay awake and alert was clearly a lesson in irony. However, I found it interesting. More interesting than some, it seemed. As usual, questions were asked to reinforce our learning, and more often than not the Unsmiling Assassin would question, pause, nominate one of the eager-eyed students keen to impress.

'So to recap then, why do we stay awake?' The Unsmiling Assassin's eyes scanned the room, searching for a willing, or unwilling, volunteer to answer.

I tried to look alert by perking up my head in an attempt to garner his attention.

'Right, just a minute fellas.' He walked from behind his lectern. 'Am I boring you, Lofty?' he asked.

I looked to where his steely glare fell. One of the nods, Brum, (no one knew his first name, but he was from Birmingham), didn't have his head raised and certainly didn't look alert. In fact, he couldn't have done a better impression of inattentiveness if he'd tried. His chin sat on his chest, his eyes firmly closed. He seemed content enough; anyone would, emitting the sort of wheeze that suggests a sleep so deep that it's bordering clinical death.

'Don't any of you wake him up,' warned the Unsmiling Assassin as he approached Sleeping Beauty, who now had the temerity to snore.

'Oi, fuckdust, wake up.' No answer. To be fair, the corporal hadn't shouted. He never did.

'What's his name?' the Unsmiling Assassin asked the group.

'Davies, Corporal,' answered a voice from the crowd.

'Oi, Davies, you knob jockey, wake up.'

Davies still didn't move.

'Is he dead?'

Now, if you were asked how to wake somebody up in such a circumstance, or indeed check if someone was still alive, would you:

A. Give them a shake?

B. Shout at them a little louder?

C. Hit them on the head with a wooden mallet?

The Unsmiling Assassin chose the third option, picking up a large-headed mallet designed to hammer in very big tent pegs. In his defence, he didn't actually hit Davies on the head with it. He just let the natural weight of the mallet fall with a thud that drew a collective '*oof*' from the rest of us.

'Awake now are we, Princess?' asked the Unsmiling Assassin politely.

Davies, rather shell-shocked but awake, was speechless. Funnily enough, he didn't fall asleep again, probably due to pain from the large haematoma that bulged from his bonce.

We practised sentry duty that night. As the youngest I was the least important, so I was detailed to the shittiest watch. Other than contracting Ebola, it was the last thing I wanted. In the summer, doing the 03.30-04.30 watch meant finishing just prior to being called for first light stand-to. Stand-to was a call for alertness; everyone had to lie in the harbour position, in a small circle of bivvies, for forty-five minutes before both first and last light, the logic being this was the most likely time for enemy attack. For a recruit, it was also the most likely time to get a kick up the arse from the training team should we not be positioned correctly. Once the light had sufficiently changed we would then be allowed to 'stand down', and rub the aforementioned kicked arse.

My first sentry duty was textbook: alert and awake, I scanned the trees and paths in my arcs of vision. Any time there was even a hint of a rustle I'd shout, 'Halt! Who goes there?' to nothing more than the breeze. On my second sentry duty, I listened to my quick brief, laid down, got comfy and... zzzzzzzzzzz.

Luckily, there is an inner panic button we develop when asleep, a primordial survival instinct, and mine kicked in. Admittedly, it did take twenty minutes – thankfully, a short enough time not to get caught and thrashed to within an inch of my life.

I wasn't the only one to succumb to the heat of the day and general lack of sleep. One favourite trick of the trainers was to wake us from our slumber, and force us into a game of 'It Pays to Be a Winner'.

The rules were simple. On the command 'Go!' we would race over rough ground like demented maniacs to a distant object, usually a solitary tree at the top of an incline, and back to the starting point. It would have taken an Olympic athlete about a minute to complete the race, but the training team expected us all to return within half the time as a mark of 'putting effort in'. The first lad to return would be the winner and exempt from the repeat race, with the winner of each rested from the subsequent races until only the last few remained.

It certainly didn't pay to be a loser. The slower lads would run more than ten times the distance of the faster lads, and despite what the corporals said, it didn't make them any faster. It was pretty obvious who the fastest lads were, and it would have been easy not to put in 100 per cent effort for the first few races as we knew it'd be a waste of energy trying to keep up with Hopkins and the like. However, the training team was wise to the trickery of those who 'loafed', and happily dished out press-ups or star-jumps as an alternative. This slowed down the recipients even further.

Up to now, we had only worn badly-shaped blue berets and field caps. Now we were running around with helmets that seemed to be designed by that benevolent old soul Torquemada. Imagine a WWI German helmet with the point sticking out from the top: our helmets had the point protruding downwards inside the helmet. This sharp point was the male fixing for securing to the female fixing of the inner cap that looked like a Tour de France cyclist's helmet. Should the inner cap and the spike not fit properly then the spike would bounce into your skull as you ran, the stabbing pain magnified by the bounce of the elastic chinstrap. Too scared to disclose that my male and female fixings didn't fit, I winced every time I went over broken ground or had to run, which was pretty much all the time. The problem was finally noticed as we did some practice attacks, when the troop sergeant saw the blood dripping down my grid.

'Time!' he yelled. 'Get over here. You've got red sweat rolling down your face.'

He took off my helmet, checked the inside and shook his head wearily at me. 'Put some masking tape over the spike, you wanker,' he said rather unsympathetically. 'On your way.'

So off I went, being the wanker I was, continuing to bleed heavily from the incessant spearing of my helmet until late afternoon, when I could actually get hold of some mythical Harry Black Maskers which, as anyone who has ever served in the Corps will tell you, is as rare as hen's teeth.

\* \* \*

Slowly, we were turning from a collection of selfish individuals into a team. It had been hammered into us from day one, and 'I' was finally becoming 'we'. The buddy system became second nature: if I had to check that my buddy was properly dressed or feeling okay, he'd check on me too – as long as I wasn't paired with Jackie. In modern street language, we 'had each other's backs', and in the Royal Marines the bond did indeed become gang-like.

With this new-found bond, we inspected each other like chimps checking for fleas, and even when we were woken up by explosions simulating an attack and were forced to evacuate with our kit to another position, we managed to think for each other, ensuring our mates had collected their kit and were all following in the same direction.

These 'crash moves' were intended to simulate the emergency evacuation of a position. I was under the impression that, as trainee commandos, we were on the way to omnipotence and this constant crash moving was an irksome folly. Surely we'd just stand and fight, no matter how many Chinese were pouring over the hill? We only had seven hours of night routine: in crash moving three or four times a night, I dreaded the sort of conflict we could be engaged in where this would actually happen. It kept us in a constant state somewhere between somnolence and death during the heat of the day.

The lessons we were receiving, whether in the syllabus or otherwise, were harsh ones. If we didn't learn from those lessons we knew the consequences would be painful, or tiresome. But they were valuable. We learnt quickly and we learnt well – though not well enough, according to the training team.

. Being dehydrated wasn't something we needed much tutelage in. If I'd been sitting in a stripy deckchair in my vest and pants, wearing a knotted hankie on my head, I'd have required at least four litres of water. We had one warm 1.5 litre-bottle a day, of which we could actually drink very little. Fully clothed, constantly running, carrying 30kg of equipment, stressed and tired, undertaking all manner of physical activity designed to test our endurance, we were all suffering. But in week four, no-one would dare question the training team's methods.

On the final morning, all that was left to do was de-rig and pack up the training team's area. They had the privilege of using a field kitchen. Nightly, it would waft out the aroma of bacon and eggs, while we hungry recruits lived on ration packs a stone's throw away. The field kitchen's pots and pans required a serious clean before returning to the stores back at Lympstone. I was one of five detailed to the washing up. With no hot water, the washing-up liquid was used with gay abandon, but did the trick sufficiently. With only hydration on my mind, I blew the excess bubbles from the top of the large bowl and drank a ladle full of greasy, fetid water, to the hilarity of the other four.

'What's it taste like?' asked Brum Davies, still nursing a lump the size of a crème caramel on his head.

'It's quite nice,' I replied.

'Really?'

'Yeah, it's a bit meaty, like Bovril.'

'Give us a go then,' Davies took a large swig and spurted it out all over himself. 'It tastes like shit.'

'Uh, yes,' I replied, and realised it had taken me until the last day of week four to take the piss out of someone. My confidence had grown.

Although ghastly, it quenched my parched throat, so I took another ladle full. Noting my ability not to throw up, the others followed suit, even Davies reluctantly drank more with his nose pinched. It was a great opportunity to rehydrate, until one of the corporals noted our high-spirited drinking party. He ended proceedings by kicking me in the kidneys for being a stupid prick and poisoning myself. But by this time we'd all drank our fair share of greasy, dirty sullage.

Packing finished, we sat expectantly, under the shade of one of Woodbury Common's many copses, for the four-tonne truck to bus us back to CTC.

'Right fellas, listen in.' said the Unsmiling Assassin. 'The transport was due to be here by now, but one of the things you may not know about the road between CTC and Woodbury Common is that it is like the Bermuda Triangle. Looks like your truck has been swallowed up. What a bastard eh? So what alternatives do we have to get back then?'

We all knew, but really didn't want to say.

'Wait for another one?' asked Jackie hopefully. It was going to be his last day so idiotic questions weren't really an issue for him.

'Unfortunately, we can't afford to lose any more four-tonners. Only one way to go, and that's by Shanks's pony. We do know what that is, don't we?'

With the other corporals lined up with all their kit on their backs, we had a good idea.

'Right, three ranks in front of me, go!'

From the serenity of basking in the shade of summer trees we were catapulted into a maelstrom of activity and within a minute we were ready, fully kitted in three ranks, already sweating like huskies in a sauna.

'One of the commando tests is a nine-mile speed march, guys,' added Corporal Stevens from the flank. 'This is a piece of piss. It's only eight.'

We were already exhausted from a week of sleep deprivation. Speed marching for the first time with the 30kg of kit on our backs, in the middle of a hot summer's day, elicited auditory signals of struggle.

'Shitten it. Stop feeling sorry for yourself,' Corporal Stevens answered one particular grunt of anguished exhaustion.

By halfway, the troop had split in two. Near the end, the divisions had become greater, as too had the shouting of the training team running alongside.

'Pain is just weakness leaving the body, fellas,' shouted one corporal.

'It doesn't hurt when the pain has gone,' screamed another, continuing the theme.

By the time we reached CTCRM, only around fifteen of us had finished as a lead group. It was noted that all five of us on washing-up detail had finished. It was also the first time I had been told, 'Well done.'

\* \* \*

Three weeks of summer leave followed. Everywhere I went, I wore my Royal Marines sweatshirt with pride amongst my old schoolmates who were either on Youth Training Schemes or, God forbid, still at school. They needed to get out into the real world. I had been a Royal Marines recruit for four weeks and done things they would never dream of (like boot-polishing a floor with a toothbrush).

They questioned me relentlessly about the mystical world into which I'd disappeared, and I was only too happy to fuel their imagination with awe-inspiring tales of heroism, despite experiencing very little of it. I sat in a café with an old schoolmate drinking coffee, and managed to catch a fly that had been annoying me.

'Did you learn that in the Marines?' he said, eyes popping at my killing skills.

I could have blown his mind by replying, 'Yes, week three in training was devoted to catching flying insects.' But instead I just smiled and said, 'My reflexes have sharpened up a bit.'

And maybe they had. Despite being a Royal Marine recruit for only four weeks, a few days of rest had left me feeling sharper, stronger and fitter than I'd ever been. But my feet were a real problem. Permanently blistered, my heels were raw; an area of skin the size of a fifty-pence piece had worn away, leaving me in total agony when walking in anything other than a pair of slippers, which unfortunately were not a military-issue item. At least on leave I could go back to wearing nice, soft trainers to ease the pain and hopefully allow them to heal.

Noting my pain, and horrified at the state of my feet, my

mam suggested pissing on them. This surprised me. I'd found pornography hidden in my stepdad's wardrobe but I didn't think they'd gone that far. But apparently it was an old miner's trick to harden the hands and prevent blistering.

With only two short planks of common sense between my ears, I thought I'd give it a go. Pissing on my heels was easy enough, but trying to get the outsides of my ankles was decidedly more difficult. Whichever way I contorted my body, legs and rather inadequate penis, it was impossible.

Please have a go sometime, or, by way of a comparison, try this: next time you go to a garden fete, visit the Scouts' stall. They will undoubtedly have that piss-poor game where you trail a metal hoop along a twisting length of electrified wire, trying not to make the spotty little twat in charge laugh at you when the wire buzzes as the hoop touches and you lose your 10p. When you've finished punching his specky face, nick the game and take it home, where you can begin the following experiment:

Erect a stepladder in the doorway adjoining the dining room and the kitchen.

Saw an inch from one leg on the dining-room side and cover it in creosote, balancing the ladder so it doesn't touch the new wholemeal carpet in your dining room.

Place the opposite legs on the kitchen linoleum, on upturned margarine wrappers.

The fourth and untouched leg can be left alone. (The more advanced can place it on an upturned treacle can.)

Place a comedy mirror in your kitchen, preferably one that makes your head look the size of an old 7" single.

Strap the wire game to the top of your head using black masking tape.

Climb to the top rung of the stepladder (the one the instructions tell you not to stand on).

Now look into the comedy mirror and try to drag the hoop successfully around the wire without leaving a creosote stain on your carpet from unbalancing the ladder.

That takes *half* the skill needed to urinate on the outsides of your ankles.

I tried it in the bath without a flat surface. It wasn't at all surprising when, with one foot planted on the opposite thigh, I slipped. Thrusting out my arms, I grabbed the shower curtain and wrenched the pole from its fixing, crashing to the floor in a snotty heap. My mother heard the racket, and rushed in to see what on earth I'd done. There I lay, my meat and two veg flaccidly parading, semi-wrapped in a floral shower curtain with a pole across my head.

'I was trying to piss on my blisters,' I said, 'but I couldn't reach the sides of my ankles. I slipped.'

'Why didn't you just pee on your hand and rub it in?' she said.

IQ 150, common sense zero.

This may have been why my ankle blisters didn't heal very well. Mind you, neither did the ones on my heels. They looked just as bad, but smelled a lot pissier.

* * *

So eager was I to get back to training that I returned two days early – a ridiculous idea, as CTCRM only had a skeleton staff and most of the camp was closed. I spent forty-eight hours stuck in my room, scared shitless as the accommodation block took on a spooky aura when empty.

The first week back at CTC took off as it had finished: lots of shouting, weapons training, physical exercise, and cleaning. Jackie and five others had dropped out. They returned all the way to camp to immediately put in their notice to opt out, and within the next day or two they were never to be seen again. Within five weeks we had lost nearly thirty per cent of the troop.

Being sixteen and therefore still classed as a child – although not treated like one, unless you count the Victorian workhouses – I was issued a third of a pint of milk daily that would be sent to the training team's office. The office sat in the corner of the accommodation block's landing and should have had a yellow and black cordon tape reading, 'CAUTION: BASTARDS AT WORK.'

Going to the training team's office was as nerve-wracking as meeting the Queen –though the Queen would probably not call me a 'scrote'.

The story goes – and I can totally believe it – that a nervous recruit, already in the shit for some hideous misdemeanour, such as having a difficult-to-pronounce surname, knocked on the training team's door. Despite him knowing for certain they were inside, there was no answer. He knocked again, and waited like a forlorn puppy for attention. When he had been standing there for two minutes, a corporal opened the door. Inside sat the whole team, with the troop sergeant busy making a noose to scare the nods.

'What do you want, scrote? It had better be important. I'm busy,' says the troop sergeant.

'Yes, it is, Sar…'

The corporal at the door interjects, 'Is that how you report to the troop sergeant, fuckdust? Get out and report properly.'

So the recruit smartly about-turns and leaves the office. Halting, he about-turns again to have the door slammed in his face like a gypsy offering to tarmac a drive.

He knocks again. No answer. He knocks again.

The door opens and the corporal instructs the recruit to report.

The nod marches back in properly, clashing his heels together to attention.

The sergeant says, 'Right, let's start again.'

'Sergeant, I am PO45740J Tumblefish. Permission to speak, Sergeant.'

'That's better. Now, what do you want?'

'Sergeant, my room is on fire.'

So it was with trepidation that I'd knock every morning to receive my milk. And every morning I found the milk had already been used as a welcome addition to their morning's teas and coffees. I was sure it was my only contribution to the training team's happiness, and the main reason I was still with the troop.

By now we were allowed off camp, so we were ordered to the training team's office to be issued a shore-leave pass. It was probably the only time we ever wanted to visit the team office.

'Time!' shouted Corporal Stevens from within the office. I marched in as well as I could with my shitty feet.

'It says here, "Junior Marine." How old are you, Time?' he asked, the shore-leave pass waving in front of my eyes.

'Sixteen, Corporal.'

'Have you been out on your own after six o'clock?'

I returned his smirk. 'Yes, Corporal.'

'Probably out in the park drinking cider, weren't you?' he added. He didn't realise how close to the truth he was.

'No, Corporal,' I smirked again.

'You are not to drink when you're ashore, Time.'

'Of course not, Corporal.' My smirk suggested I thought he was joking, but his deadpan glare definitely suggested otherwise.

'If I find out you've been drinking you will be charged. Do you hear me?'

The lightheartedness had turned menacing. I had no doubt he was a man of his word. It was quite okay for him to teach me how to kill people, but God forbid I might order a Babycham.

Despite Royal Marine camps being on dry land, getting off camp and into the civilian community was known as 'going ashore'. As a recruit, it was an exercise in itself.

Most of the accommodation blocks were around 100m from the train platform. But we'd have to trek 400m in the opposite direction up to the Guard Room at the main gate to join a queue more suited to popular theme-park rides. Once at the front of the queue you would report and ask the duty guard commander, 'Permission to go ashore.' As part of the ceremony, the guard commander would then inspect us before we trekked the 500m back to the train stop.

Inspection for going ashore gave *carte blanche* to the bored guard commanders, pissed off that they were working weekends, to deny you permission. Rejection could be for any odd reason and given with equally bizarre explanations.

Wearing white socks:

'Who do you think you are, John Travolta?'

Trousers too short:

'Put some jam on your shoes to attract them down.'

Laces twisted:

'If you were in the First World War you'd have been stabbed in the trenches.'

Or you had a weird accent:

'Come back in ten minutes and talk properly.'

Pushed for time as we were, any rejection meant running back to the accommodation to fix socks/trousers/laces/speech, before running back to the guardroom to queue up again for more ridicule, in the vain hope you'd catch the next freedom train out.

With uniform haircuts, polished shoes, trousers (recruits were not allowed to be wear jeans) and pressed shirts, we were not only recognisable as nods walking around Exeter but obvious targets for the IRA and, more probably, the fashion police. We all frequented the same pubs. One, The Turk's Head, was known as 'The Nod's Head'. On any given Saturday afternoon you'd think you had walked in on a skinheads' 'how to dress smartly and talk in abbreviations' convention. If your leave pass allowed you out late, you'd then move on to Tens nightclub – a dark, sticky-carpeted, subterranean nightspot full of easily-pissed recruits desperate for even the smell of a girl's neck perfume, and even more inebriated women more than happy to allow recruits to smell wherever they wanted.

While encouraged to go out in Exeter, an evening in nearby Exmouth was strictly off limits to nods. It was the domain of trained ranks and training teams. An afternoon visit to promenade along the seafront was allowed, but if a nod was caught in a pub it was seen as a show of insolence and a quiet word would be had, along to the lines of, 'Off is the general direction in which I wish you to fuck.'

The nod would then disappear in the direction of Exeter, usually with a chit attached to his forehead saying, 'Please beast me first thing Monday morning.'

An afternoon ashore would usually consist of wandering aimlessly around the shops, not really buying anything of use to the layperson apart from the odd music cassette. We nods regularly found ourselves in outward bounds suppliers, buying yet more green string in case the twenty metres in our holdalls got used or lost. I reckon if I had opened a green string shop in Exeter (probably called something like Geez String!) I'd have been able to retire by now.

Occasionally, if you were confident of staying awake in the dark, you might catch a film. One time, Hopkins, the lads and I went to watch Sly Stallone in *Cobra*. Prior to joining up, I'd been refused entry to watch *Commando*, even though I was about to become one. As I queued up I reflected that as a serviceman, a government-trained assassin with a lust for napalm and hot chicks, I'd surely be allowed in this time. But no, I was relegated to watching the 15-rated *Ferris Bueller's Day Off*. And I still got my ID checked beforehand.

I had the last laugh, though. The general assessment was that *Cobra* was shite, and I'd had a narrow escape. It was probably the only time when being so young was an advantage.

# SIX

*'My blood congeals, and I can write no more.'*

DR FAUSTUS – CHRISTOPHER MARLOWE

THERE ARE MANY old stories that abound in Royal Marines folklore. Indeed, this 'dit' culture of storytelling is part of the Corps ethos. Some may be factual, some a little embellished and some a total fabrication. Whatever the level of veracity, 'spinning dits' has become an important factor in underpinning the character of a Royal Marine, whether the story is set at the Battle of Trafalgar or in The Battle of Trafalgar pub.

A DL inspects a recruit troop on the drill square at CTC. The recruits have their dry weapons stripped down and, as per usual, the DL ensures there is not even a gnat's hair present.

He looks through the weapon barrel of one recruit and spots something within the rifling. He passes the weapon to the recruit for him to look through.

'What can you see through there, Lofty?' asks the DL.

The nod looks closely up through the barrel. 'The officers' mess, Corporal.'

Whether or not it is true, just the presence of an officers' mess at CTC is unique. The Army has Sandhurst as an academy to train its officers, the Royal Navy has Britannia Royal Naval College in Dartmouth, and the RAF probably trains its officers at the Ritz for a couple of weeks before heading off on a skiing trip.

The Royal Marines make no such distinction in training establishments, and therefore officer recruits – Young Officers, or YOs – while living in the mess, mingle with non-commissioned recruits on a daily basis, undertaking similar lectures in the same areas, receiving the same level of instruction. This not only provides an instant bond between a Royal Marines officer and his men, but also offers a recruit an insight into the lives of their future commanders, with less of the separation often prevalent in the other services.

A Royal Marines officer on a course at an army barracks is in the mess eating breakfast with officers from all arms of the services. He asks a Guards officer, busy reading the morning's broadsheet across the other side of the dinner table, 'Could you please pass the salt?'

The Guards officer ignores the request, so the RM officer repeats it.

The Guards officer looks up. 'Are you aware that when a Guards officer is reading the newspaper it means he does not want to be disturbed?'

The Royal Marines officer pauses before climbing onto

the dinner table and stamping into a bowl, kicking milk and cereal all over the Guards officer's newspaper and uniform.

'Are you aware that when a Royal Marines officer stands in your cornflakes it means pass the fucking salt?'

Again, this is possibly an embellishment of the truth, but it does show how rough around the edges the typical bootneck officer is. Which could not be said about one YO who arrived to commence training.

The press was constantly parked outside the main gate as if some B-list celebrity had been seen entering. We had been told by the camp hierarchy to stay away from them; as if we had time to go up to the main gate and start a conversation with anyone; as if we could even get out of the main gate. Even when ashore journalists would approach us, keen to get a scoop from some young nod with a head full of wild stories about our new Young Officer: His Royal Highness Prince Edward.

We had known of his arrival on return from summer leave. While quite thrilling for many, I'd have taken his presence with a huge dollop of ambivalence if it wasn't for the fact that his academic qualifications were shit and his presence was based upon birthright and not merit. Regressing to my socialist roots, I thought his commission only denied someone more deserving.

I saw him only on occasion, the rosy red cheeks on his otherwise pasty face giving him a permanent look of embarrassment and adding to an androgyny that would make him popular if he ever ended up in prison. I do recall he wore a very badly-shaped beret like a felt cushion on his head, and in truth he didn't look at all like a bootneck officer. Never once did I see him smile and I certainly never saw him pissing in a doorway. The PR gurus at CTC told the press that Prince Edward would be treated just like everyone else going through training, so I was at a loss as to why I never had two bodyguards by my side when I went ashore to buy green string.

* * *

The military was going through kit and equipment changes in 1986. We were to be issued the new Mk 6 nylon fibre helmet, which we were told was the best thing since sliced bread. I would have preferred sliced bread on my head.

As we were some of the first troops to be issued this new-fangled head protector, logistical problems meant the first shipments only came in one size: Extra Fucking Large. Unfortunately, those of us who didn't have a noggin the size of a beach ball ended up looking like an overgrown toadstool.

The new MK6 helmet also came with a camouflaged DPM cover. Logistical problems also meant the first shipments only came in one size: Extra Fucking Small. To get it over the helmet was like trying to put a baby cap over an Atlas stone and our initial attempts were failures, raising the ire of the DL who didn't want his troops to wear helmets that seemed to turn them into the Hulk.

The DL attempted to fit the cover over the helmet as proof it could be done. With the laws of physics not assisting his argument, he advised us to soak the covers in cold water then give them a good stretch. As always, we did what he said, which in retrospect may have been a mistake.

When I was a child there were toys that you could put in water and they would grow exponentially. I think they were eventually banned as a child swallowed one and it expanded in his stomach until he died. The MK6 helmet cover was the exact opposite of that banned toy: once it was placed in water it shrunk as if it was in a film called *Honey, I Shrunk My Helmet Cover*.

In no part could we be blamed for the logistical fuck-ups, yet all this ill-sized equipment only led to more beastings. As we were now issued weapons, the beastings could take on a different shade of agony. Stress positions, although deemed ill-treatment by the UN, were an active participation sport at CTC and combined with shoot-to-kill exercises that sounded very Ramboesque, but in reality were painful isometrics where we'd hold the weapon at various degrees of discomfort for a long time, until our bodies could take little more.

The SLR only weighed just over 4kg, but its length meant holding it horizontal with one arm for the duration of an episode of *Coronation Street* was as painful as listening to Deidre Barlow. Shoot-to-kill exercises could be undertaken anywhere due to their static nature, so you didn't even need space. I even got roped into one after having a piss with my weapon slung over my shoulder, as I'd earlier been seen taking my milk outside the training team office. According to Corporal Stevens, consuming the milk would make holding the weapon out to the side far easier. It didn't.

\* \* \*

Week five morphed into week six that seamlessly turned into week seven. Characters came and went, as new guys joined from troops ahead of us. These 'back troopers' could have been injured, therefore undergoing a rehabilitative period, or failed a criteria test, meaning they would have to be sent back to the appropriate week of training. Being back trooped was a humiliation whatever the reason, and it was the sword of Damocles that hung over the head of every recruit that passed through training. With the ever-changing faces, closeness towards back troopers was sometimes a little strained, as if a family member had been replaced by a strange interloper, accepted warily until proving his worth.

This unease wasn't helped by the spate of thefts that occurred within the troop. This was an immensely destructive element in such a tight-knit group, creeping into everyone's psyche as well as their belongings to pilfer not only money but trust.

Indeed, I was accused at one point. I had walked into a room to look for Hopkins, only to be surprised by another recruit lying on his bed, hidden behind his locker. He jumped to the conclusion that I was there to steal. Other than being accused of paedophilia, or of supporting Manchester United, I can't think of any worse accusation, and I was happy to tell him so in such a manner that we had to be pulled apart by other recruits.

The thief was winning. Despite my protestations of innocence, I knew that fingers would be secretly pointed.

The Special Investigations Branch (SIB) was called in to take fingerprints of everyone in the troop. While this was humiliating, I knew it would exonerate me when the real culprit was unearthed.

\* \* \*

Most of our outdoor training was conducted on the coarse heaths of Woodbury Common. A dog walker's paradise, the scrub of the heath was crisscrossed by the many rough firebreaks that turned ankles and shredded skin if we fell. We tended not to use these firebreaks all that often, preferring the small tracks that were the capillary routes between the different areas of training. Mostly though, we were either on our backs, fronts or knees within the heath itself, a thick web of gorse and thickets that pulled, nipped and slapped us like a public-school flogging every time we tried stalking – in layperson's parlance 'creeping up on the enemy', one of the core skills of a sniper.

I thought I'd be good at stalking. As a small child I often went strawberry nicking after the fields were closed to the public. I would, in military terms, 'leopard crawl', using the strawberry mounds as cover and secretively eating as many as I could until the nausea of overindulgence took over. Only once did I ever get caught. Trying to flee from a farmer's salt pellet-filled shotgun with the weight of a hundred strawberries swilling around my stomach led to me vomiting red sick down my front. My gran thought I'd been shot in the face.

I also thought being a short-arse would be an advantage,

but never realised that, once laid down, we're all pretty much the same height. I usually did well on the stalking stances, although with my inclination to chance things a little further I'd often be caught trying to get too close, which would result in a bollocking as bad as for those seen from a huge distance. There was no need for me to get so close and blow my cover. Carrying a weapon with a battle range of 300m, there was little point in getting to 60m and being shot. In any case, it meant less time spent crawling amongst the painful undergrowth.

This permanent contact with the gorse often resulted in many recruits developing the infamous 'Woodbury rash'. With bodies worn down by perpetual activity, it thrived on our lowered immune systems, leaving skin looking like bubble wrap and each pore a yellow pustule. Like many, my spare time was often taken up by squeezing, repeatedly amazed at what the zits would offer. It was like opening up a Kinder Surprise egg, only I wouldn't be rewarded with a dodgy toy, but with pus, blood and, if especially lucky, a gorse needle.

The thighs and knees took the brunt, but some recruits found the rash on their arse, which left a nice dot-to-dot puzzle for anyone brave enough to complete. Some even suffered symptoms on their genitalia, although this could have been a questionable excuse. A few would suffer huge black boils akin to the bubonic plague, and would be immobilised or back trooped due to severe infection.

Years later, a Royal Marine recruit would die from the rash and was soon followed by an elderly woman who passed away from a single scratch. Studies showed that the gorse itself can cause a Group A streptococcal infection, which can lead to all manner of nasty diseases. So, although the most dangerous thing we had knowingly faced was a pusser's pasty, we were unknowingly being attacked by deadly flora that should have made a guest appearance as a *Doctor Who* baddie.

While up on Woodbury Common, we would often be handed a bag ration. Probably not named after the 18th century Georgian Prince Pyotr Ivanovich Bagration, a 'bagrat', as it was commonly known, was the lunchtime meal issued when troops were not on camp, usually in a non-tactical environment. Just as well really, as the bagrat consisted of the noisiest snacks known to humanity.

The brown bag itself was made of a paper so thin that, even if the air turned a little humid, or condensation built up on a nearby water bottle, the bottom would rot to pulp and allow all its contents to fall out. Eating a packet of crisps is about as quiet as the Hiroshima bomb and the rustle or crunch seemed to amplify in quieter surroundings. If we were lucky the crisps would be soft due to celebrating the second birthday past their best-before date.

A juice box was our refreshment, with a straw that could never pierce the silver circle and necessitated the use of a knife, resulting in clothes dowsed with sticky juice to become a target for any flying insect within a mile radius. Should you actually manage to get the straw in, the echoing slurps of reaching the bottom of the box would make the crisp packet rustling seem like a lullaby in comparison. The chocolate bar always was the ying to a ratpack 'Rolos' yang. Always melted, amazingly even in the winter, I can only assume they must have been kept in the oven prior to being bagged up, leaving the consumption making for a messy tongue wrestle with the wrapper.

The fruit would usually be an orange or apple that looked as though it had just it'd returned from fighting at a football match: battered, bruised and with chunks often missing. The sandwich would be even worse. Only eaten to stave off starvation, the selection was immense: cheese and pickle, or polony and pickle. The cheese would be wafer thin or as thick as a brick, depending of on the boredom level of the sandwich maker, or the cheapest of polonies where visible pieces of a pig's mutilated cock or eyelid, complete with lashes, were as prevalent as the bits of bone. On occasion we could hit the jackpot and even find a small amount of meat. For whatever reason, possibly in the name of being 'continental', the polony would often have a circle of stuffing in the middle. The contents of that stuffing were something known to only the guardians of Area 51 but at a guess it was a mix of cigarette ash, bum fluff and sage. In the meat processing factory, I can only suggest that there are three conveyors graded 'Fit for Human Consumption', 'Unfit for Human Consumption' and 'Food for Royal Marines'. In normal circumstances, guys on restricted privileges usually made the bagrats, so their culinary pride was hardly on a par with Fanny Craddock, making eating any sandwich a cautious lucky dip.

As if training and stomaching a bagrat wasn't hard enough, those recruits who didn't come up to scratch in their personal administration were either charged or put on 'crabby recruit routine'. To be put onto 'crabby' was a fate worse than death. Not only were you ordered to parade five extra times in every uniform that you held, you were tainted as being 'dirty'. The fact that those on 'crabby' were godly clean compared to civilians was irrelevant. Even being found with a stone embedded into the sole of a polished boot in a clean locker could be sufficient reason to find oneself on crabby recruit routine. By Royal Marines standards they were lepers: dirty, filthy tramps who were pariahs to the mainstream recruits. Fortunately, my administration was of sufficient standard. However, on a week-eight exercise called Hunter's Moon I was found out.

Piss-wet through all week, the exercise was a continual trial of yomping from one harbour position to another, interspersed with practising our map-reading skills, camouflage and concealment for stalking activities, and observation stances where we would try to find a water bottle hiding in a bush or a torch sneakily tucked behind a tree. The October rain – 'It's not rain, it's liquid sunshine,' we were told – let up for around two hours on the Wednesday night, but that was irrelevant as we were being crash moved yet again, dragging all our saturated kit through the mud of Woodbury Common. On the Thursday morning, with little sleep, yet another field inspection was scheduled.

I was extra tired, truly hanging out of my hoop. That night I had been on sentry and Hopkins was my relief. As per normal, ten minutes before the end of my watch I'd scramble through the bivvies, having noted previously where he'd be. The harbour position always looked different in the wooded blackness and any of us could trip over bivvies and bits of errant kit, or just fall into holes in the ground. I eventually found him.

'Hopkins, your turn for sentry,' I whispered.

'Nah mate, wrong bivvy. I woke you up.'

This was a usual ploy and one I'd tried before getting kicked for it. Some had even denied who they were, preferring instead to get a precious five more minutes sleep while the confused recruit bimbled around looking for them, then realised he'd been correct all along.

'No, Elliott woke me up. It's your turn.'

He jumped from his bivvy still wrapped in his sleeping bag.

'I'm not getting up. Fuck off.'

I was taken aback, this lad was supposed to be my best mate – not that I had many others to choose from. He shrivelled back into the dampness of his bivvy. He obviously didn't realise it was me.

'It's me, Timey. Mate, you okay? You can't go back to sleep.' It's hard to be assertive when whispering.

'Seriously, fuck off. Leave me alone.'

Although he wasn't the happiest of fellows, he seemed to take to training with far more ease than someone like me. But here he was blatantly refusing to do his job. What could I do? I wouldn't grass him up to the training team. I certainly couldn't wake anyone else up. They were hardly going to volunteer to get up an hour early in the pouring rain to do extra sentry duty.

My only option was to return to position and do Hopkins' sentry. That feeling of smugness when just about to go to sleep had ebbed away, and here I was again with cold rain falling down the back of my neck, trickling iced water down my spine like some Devonian water torture. Looking into the blackness of pine forests, I could only wonder what the fuck was wrong with Hopkins.

I didn't manage to speak to him once stand down had been called after first light. He was keeping himself to himself behind the screen of his bivvy, saying little while eating his breakfast bacon grill from the tin.

On morning inspection being called, we hurriedly clustered together in our sections, laid out all our equipment as neatly as we could on our soaking wet ponchos, and stripped down our weapons for field conditions.

As I stood at ease behind my poncho, I looked across to the other section where the Unsmiling Assassin was on his haunches inspecting the underneath of mess tins, the cleanliness of bayonets that were never used, and checking the amount of water in bottles. Anything less than full and it would be emptied, a rather strange punishment for not having a full complement of water. The guys in his section tended to be the better recruits and we put it down to them being shit-scared of their section commander.

'Why are your boots muddy, Lofty?' asked the Unsmiling Assassin politely, as he always did.

The recruit answered with a shivering mouth, ''Cos it's… it's… muddy, Corporal.'

Yet his logical gibbering wasn't due to him being scared of the punishment that awaited – he was fucking frozen. Awaiting him were a number of ways to warm him up, none of which could be considered desirable.

The cold gnawed at my bones too. My stinging ears took note of the activity to my right as Corporal Stevens inspected my fellow section members. As he approached, nervousness rose from my stomach as it always did. I would always get picked up for something and my press-ups were legendary.

Corporal Stevens came into view with a mess tin swinging from his finger. He lobbed it into the undergrowth behind and turned to Davies who he had just inspected.

'Off you go, Davies, crawl and get it back. You can start from that puddle.'

Davies lay down next to the fetid puddle at his feet. But that was a slight understatement: it was, in fact, a large fuck-off pool of muddy water, seemingly made by the many trucks that had ploughed these soft tracks.

'Stop!' Corporal Stevens exclaimed. 'The middle of the puddle is your starting point, lightweight. Get in there and then start.'

Davies slipped onto his hands and knees into the brown water that mirrored his despondency.

'Leopard crawl, fuckwit, not monkey crawl,' added Corporal Stevens, just to make Davies' burden a little moister.

Corporal Stevens then benevolently turned his attention back to me. 'Time...'

'Good morning, Corporal.'

'Is it a good morning, Time?'

'Up to now, Corporal, yes.' My eyes did not move as he bent down to pick up my weapon.

'Hmm, well, looks like it's going to go downhill from here, then.'

The muzzle of my SLR came into my eye line as it was thrust towards my face.

'What's that there?' He motioned towards the flash eliminator, which was now an inch from my bleary eye.

I looked. Inside one of the eliminator grooves was a patch of brown.

'Cake?' I asked, more in hope than certitude.

I didn't know whether he wanted to laugh or punch my head in. 'Cake? Fucking cake?'

It was a fair response. I couldn't actually recall eating any cake during the week, let alone while cleaning my weapon. It did appear a foolhardy thing to do just in case crumbs *did* fall into the flash eliminator.

'It's fucking rust! Not fucking cake. Give me fifty.'

So while I was doing fifty very wet and heavy press-ups, and listening to Davies getting his lanyard stuck in the gorse he was crawling through, Corporal Stevens was recounting my story to the other members of the training team, asking them whether it was indeed ginger or Dundee cake while levelling a variety of quite offensive names at me.

'You realise a rusty weapon is a chargeable offence, numpty bollocks?' said Corporal Stevens after I'd finished my press ups.

I did now. On my return to camp, not only had I learnt a new phrase of abuse, but was marched into the company commander's office to be lectured on the importance of my weapon being clean. I was to be charged £50 – a week's wage – and seven days restricted privileges (RPs), which meant I could not go ashore at the weekend. I just hoped I'd stocked up on enough green string.

As if I wasn't busy enough, having RPs meant I now had

to report to the guardroom at 06.00, 18.00, and 22.00 in my half-lovat uniform, to be inspected and lectured about weapons cleanliness by the bored guard commander who was probably pissed off that my presence took him away from him watching television.

'Here you go, Lofty, just to confirm you have understood what I've said you can give me a confirmatory demonstration on how to clean,' said the guard commander, throwing me some rags and a tin of Brasso. 'For the next half an hour you can busy yourself by making those cannons glisten.'

I looked at the cannons that flanked the guardroom door. How I was to make them glisten even more I didn't know. But I gave it a good go.

'Right, that's half an hour, Lofty. Let's see how we've got on, shall we?' said the guard commander, probably during the TV advert breaks.

I'd rubbed the brass cannons so hard I was surprised a genie hadn't appeared. But to me, the before and after shots were the same.

To the corporal, who had super commando eyesight, the cannons appeared to be shit. 'Have you been sat on your arse out here doing fuck all?'

I had been sat on my arse, that was true, but doing fuck all could hardly be confused with furious polishing.

'You've got another fifteen minutes before you can stand down. These cannons better be a far sight better or you can stay another hour.' With that warning he returned to watch the second half of *Blockbusters*, or whatever else was on.

I recommenced my polishing with the same gusto as a

masturbating convict. After the additional fifteen minutes I stood back to admire my work. The extra polishing still left them identical to when I started, the only difference being the mirrored reflection of a setting sun. My work seemed futile.

*Blockbusters* had obviously finished. 'Right, let's have another look,' said the guard commander, tensing his biceps as if he'd just risen from his bed. 'That's better, see what happens when you put the effort in?'

Now that he had determined the cannons were glistening acceptably, I returned to my grot knowing that at 22.00 I would be doing it all again, just in the dark.

Despite all this bullshit, these lessons were important ones. Before I could become a commando I had to become a good soldier. Before I could become a good soldier I had to get the basics right, and keeping my weapon clean was part of the ABC of soldiering.

\* \* \*

Post-exercise admin was always a day of drudgery, and after Hunter's Moon we had to work extra hard to ensure every single item of kit was emptied, scrubbed inside and out, washed, dried and then, if necessary, ironed. The metal ablutions sinks was busy with the sounds of webbing clanging against metal, boots sprayed with hot water and nailbrushes scrubbing anything with even a suggestion of mud.

With my scrubbed boots in the drying room I went to check how they were doing, like a chef assessing his rising Yorkshire puddings. The drying room was a small, dark, dank-smelling place where heated radiators made it warmer than most, and an ideal hiding spot for recruits on night duty during the winter. On entering, I found Hopkins sat cross-legged with his boots in front of him. He was crying. I had never seen a fully grown man cry before. I was clueless as to what to do, so I just stood pathetically with a mouth that wanted to say something but a head that held back.

'You okay?' It was the best I could do.

He splayed his hands in front of him. 'Someone has nicked the paper out of my boots,' he cried.

I thought he was joking. Crying over the theft of newspaper we put in our boots to quicken the drying process?

'Why would someone do that?'

I had no idea, so I offered him the paper from mine.

'It's no use, they're ruined now.'

I was becoming even more confused. Over the last couple of weeks Hopkins had become ever more withdrawn. Since leave I could count on one hand how many times he had actually laughed, despite my 'What's blue and white and lives in a tree?' joke. (It's a fridge in a denim jacket, by the way).

I sat down and faced him, also cross-legged. If disturbed now, we might have been mistaken for two lovers missing the tranquillity of solitude. It was clear he had suffered enough. He had mentioned to his father while on leave that his heart wasn't in the military, but his father insisted that most found the first few weeks of military training the most difficult and in four weeks he can't have decided whether or not it was right for him. Pressurised to return, he was another four weeks further on and still knew it wasn't for him.

I had to bow down in admiration of him. We had been thrashed night and day and he was still there, unlike the many that had decided it was all a bit too much and left. Yet Hopkins was only a sideshow in his own mini-tragedy. His competency, fitness and character were never in question, but he had suffered for his selfless obligation to family tradition without the will to find his own path. Without willpower, no matter how switched on a recruit may be, completing Royal Marines training is a near-impossible task and Hopkins was evidently past his breaking point.

He then confided that he had bought four packs of paracetamol the previous weekend from numerous chemists to avoid suspicion. He had swallowed thirty before he puked them all back up, his body rejecting the chemical that was included for that very purpose.

I listened intently. It was a cry for help. Here was I, the only emotional response given in my life so far was to pretend to cry holding a comatose Snow White in a school play (I was typecast as a dwarf) and now I was listening to someone who had tried to take his own life.

We talked for an age until we decided that he should see the Padre, the military conduit to God. I wasn't a religious man but I knew he'd have the empathy that was missing from the training team, something someone of Hopkins' disposition really needed.

It was a Friday afternoon. On Monday morning, Hopkins was on a one-way train back home, to the surprise of everyone including the training team.

# SEVEN

'We're something, aren't we? The only animals that shove things up their ass for survival.'

*PAPILLON* BY HENRI CHARRIÈRE

THE INTENSITY OF military training didn't let up. Indeed, it became harder as week nine turned to week ten. Days were long and nights were short. A typical day would commence at 05.30:

*The alarm wakes me instantly. As usual I wake in the same position that I had fallen asleep, my Walkman headphones still covering my ears. It is as if within my deep sleep subliminal messages have been constantly transmitting, 'Do not crease sheets, do not crease sheets.' My aching body seems to weigh more, increasing the*

*difficulty of rising from the mattress that, while cheap
and nasty, always fulfils its purpose. A shit, shower and
shave is the morning ritual, a precursor to the scientific
rebuild of my bedding, prior to drawing our weapons
from the armoury. It hardly caters to its clients; it is only
open between 06.30 and 07.30, forcing us to stand in a
long, but swift moving, queue.*

*Weapons secured in lockers, we run to the galley to get
breakfast along with the other thousand or so recruits –
cue more queuing. Shuffling forward in the never-ending
scran queue is often the only time we don't get hassle
so it's an opportune time to look over the balcony to
observe the other nods. I recognise who is ahead of us in
training. Which week exactly, I don't know, but I know
they are nearer the end and wonder how they managed to
survive through the weeks we have yet to face. It is easy,
amidst the smell of grease and disinfectant, the rattle of
crockery and hubbub of amalgamated chatter, to see the
sea of nods below as clones. We have the same crew-cut
haircuts and wear the same, possibly differently coloured,
Royal Marines sweatshirts or T-shirts. Variations of this
are tops reading, 'God Is A Para' and adorned on the
back, 'He Failed The Commando Course.' Other pacifist
slogans such as 'Peace Through Superior Firepower' and
'UZI Does It' are also popular.*

*After wolfing down a full-fat English breakfast with
added grease, we return to the accommodation to start
the accommodation chores. Emptying bins, sweeping,
waxing and polishing the floors with an uncontrollably*

*demonic buffing machine that dents every metal surface it careers into, leaving a mirror-like finish, so too the boot-polished ablution floor that is squeakily dry after scrubbing the toilets and showers. Even if we don't have enough time – and we rarely do – weapons are given a quick once over, the barrel pulled through and the working parts quickly and lightly oiled for any snap inspection that the training team invariably give whether we use the weapons or not. At around 07.45, the training team members are heard in their office, laughing and joking, and drinking my milk, then, like attendees at a schizophrenics' conference, turn into shouting, screaming banshees.*

*'Stand by your beds!' shouts one of the team.*

*The command echoes through the halls so we speedily return to our personal bed space and stand like guardsmen on parade, hearts pumping in nervous anticipation to await inspection. Depending on what mood the team is in, the inspection could be a cursory glance (which, although quick, is annoying – we feel we have done all this preparation for nothing), or a full-blown white glove inspection where any micro-particle of dust found is greeted with evil glee. With a dusty finger the corporal will look up triumphantly and ask, 'What's this?'*

*Many times I have wanted to say, 'It's your finger.' But obviously I don't want to be thrown from the second-floor window like many of the clothes that are hurled when the team decides to go nuclear.*

*As usual, our inspection hasn't gone well. We are*

*ordered out onto the landing where we are told in no uncertain terms, the error of our ways. Yet again, we are told to 'stand by to stand by'.*

*We undertake all this before the day's work has even started. First up for the day is a map-reading lecture where we go over lessons learnt previously. The instructor no longer shouts, but acts more as a schoolteacher, just with more obscene tattoos and an endearing humour that makes even the most mundane lectures enjoyable. Map reading over, we dash over to the other side of 'Puzzle Palace', the aptly-named large instruction block that has its lecture rooms numbered in an order that no one has yet figured out. The ten minutes between lectures are taken up by trying to find the correct room. We then take another hour to understand the troop tactics lesson given by one of the other section corporals, who absorbs the class in fantastic tales of his experiences in the Falklands conflict, strongly reinforcing the aims of his lecture.*

*Lesson over, we dream of having a 'stand easy'; the fifteen-minute break that is programmed into the daily schedule. However, a 'stand easy' is a mythical time where no one has ever been; perhaps C.S. Lewis should have named his book* The Lion, the Witch and the Stand Easy. *The fifteen minutes has been taken up by getting quickly changed into our IMF gym kit, quickly inspecting each other for specks of fluff, or twisted laces. We then run as a troop over to the gym, where again we get inspected, then put through our paces by PTIs intent on inflicting enough pain to ensure we're 'working hard enough'. Reddened and sweating like a monk in a brothel, we return to the accommodation block, quickly shower and change into the same clothes we had earlier been in to undertake another lecture, this time on first aid. The hour lunch break, as per usual, is only half that; preparation for the next period takes a good while, especially if weapons are involved, as we know an inspection awaits.*

*Often the afternoon will be spent outdoors. This is always better than being sat in a stuffy classroom where post-lunch stupor could be the death knell for us all. Permanently tired, we look like narcoleptics, nodding away while trying to take notes that start well then deteriorate to a doctor's prescription. This perpetual nodding of heads is probably the reason Royal Marine recruits are known as 'nods' and we certainly live up to the reputation. In these stuffy lecture rooms we learn a new skill: sleeping while standing up. I have seen this skill demonstrated a few times. Nods falling asleep during lessons are summarily told to stand up when caught out by the person conducting the lecture. This does not stop them from sleeping, however, and watching a man so tired his eyes cannot not stay open, no matter what position he happens to be in or what punishment may await, is morbidly enthralling. He could sway, wake, sway, wake, and then be overwhelmed by the urge to keel over and fall towards his desk. This is all immensely funny to watch, until it happens to me.*

*Weapons spotless, we parade at the 25m range for*

*a double period of zeroing where our weapons are personalised to our own dynamic. Despite my early struggles with weapon drills, I have now found those days chasing rabbits like a lunatic back home had been worthwhile and my accuracy is pretty good.*

*Once our weapons are sufficiently zeroed, we run back to the accommodation block, stow and secure them in our lockers before parading at the other end of camp to get into the lorries that take us up to Woodbury Common for some practical map reading, a confirmatory lesson from the morning's instruction. Lesson finished, we look forward to a trip back in the truck but as always, the transport mysteriously vanishes in between CTC and Woodbury Common. As always, Shanks's pony is our only means to make the four miles back to camp. As always, we arrive back at camp hot, sweaty, tired and behind schedule; more quick showers prepare us for weapon cleaning that has to be rushed as they have to be returned by 17.30. Dinner is always another exercise in queuing and wolfing down food as quickly as our hungry bodies allow – indigestion is always confirmation that we are sufficiently nourished – before returning to the accommodation to wash, dry and iron uniform; gloss, polish and buff parade clothes; then write up the day's notes in our folders.*

*As sometimes happens after 21.00hrs, time allows me to walk to the famous Dutchy's fast-food caravan where I religiously order the 'Captain Kirk' – a hotchpotch mixture of beans, fried egg, deep-fried sausage, and deep-*

*fried black pudding. It is a high-cholesterol nightcap that varies in price depending on how busy Dutchy the cook is. Eating Dutchy's is an important part of training and his caravan has helped more nods through training than any corporal. Having a Dutchy's is sometimes the difference between completing the next morning's PT and cramping up, unable to carry on.*

*If lucky, I go to bed by 22.30, crashing out exhausted. I am always adamant that I will listen to my Walkman. This is my time, the difference between work and play. But play never lasts past the first song. I have cassettes I have listened to a hundred times yet I don't know what tunes are on after the initial track.*

*I am awoken again this time by the door being kicked open. Rudely addressed as 'You fuckers,' we are told to get into gash PT rig and parade on the bottom field in five minutes. Sleep deprived and eyes stinging we run, hearts pumping hard, to the assault-course area where the section corporal stands. We are left in no doubt that we are the worst troop he has ever come across and the morning's inspection just proves how useless we are as a team. So now it is time to encourage us to elevate ourselves to the required standard. More crawling, rolling, sprinting and press-ups follow; all instructional techniques to improve our cleaning capabilities. Of course, we have done this many times before and the outcome is always the same. We have realised by now that when he instructs future recruits, he will use the same old line and punish them equally as hard; and the troop at the other end of the bottom field are probably getting told the same thing, but at 03.30 we never really think about the psychology of the training team, we just feel exasperated pain.*

*We are taken to the monkey bars of the assault course and hang from them over the iced water below. We hang there for as long as our grip can last, while we again get told the error of our ways. I look to the stars in an attempt to take my mind off the burning of my forearms as I try to hold on. The first splash signifies someone losing his will to grip any longer. As soon as the first one goes more and more fall into the water. I am still hanging on – the advantage of weighing so little – until, of course, I succumb to the watery sound of failure.*

*Slobbering back to the accommodation, we look like faecally incontinent pensioners, our tracksuit-bottom gussets hanging damply around our knees. We strip naked outside so as not to wet the accommodation block floor that would mean only even more cleaning after the alarm that will go off in an hour and a half; the starting pistol for us do it all over again, and again, and again.*

\* \* \*

While it was easier to get through one day at a time, we had the forthcoming month's schedule promulgated in the accommodation blocks. We would keenly read what torment lay ahead, but we also had sporting fixtures to look forward to, light relief from the pressures of military training.

Keen to prove my worth, I volunteered for the boxing

competition. I'd been more than disappointed that, during one physical training session, I wasn't allowed to join in the milling – three minutes of unskilled, arm-flailing, punching-the-fuck-out-of-each-other boxing – as I was the only junior and wasn't allowed to fight 'adults'. I wanted to fight the twat who accused me of stealing, but settled for the pleasure of seeing his face get pummelled into a ragout of blood and snot when he got a good hiding.

The annual Commando Training Centre Boxing Championship was something different. I was eligible as each of the twenty troops currently in training would enter fighters in a knockout competition, culminating in a finals night.

Probably the biggest night of the recruits' sporting calendar, the CTC finals night saw a packed gymnasium awash with recruits all baying for blood. Bloodlust was even more tangible should one of their troop brethren make it to the final.

I was one of those who made it to finals night. Not because I was a good boxer, but because there was only one other junior marine in my weight category, meaning a walkthrough to a straight final. My boxing training up to then had been ten minutes jabbing and crossing on the pads with the troop PTI, who said I was a natural. Maybe he was saying that to boost my ego, but as I prepared myself on the evening of the fight I needed all the confidence I could get.

Butterflies churned my stomach into cheese; my appetite waned so much that it was pointless worrying about the weigh-in. Through the graduated programme of Royal Marines training I'd bulked up to a massive 61kg, well below the necessary 63.5kg for the light welterweight category.

I was untrained and certainly couldn't consider myself a boxer. Boxers spar, do bag work and shadow box for months before they are allowed into the ring for a fight. Here I was, about to have my first encounter and I couldn't even skip. I knew the difference between a jab and a hook, and my childhood interest in televised boxing meant I'd seen how bobbing and weaving would be helpful in preventing a good snotting.

At least I knew I could take a punch, my stepfather saw to that. Head guards weren't even used in those good old days and the old-fashioned gloves filled with horsehair could make a mess of even the toughest face, so I was doubly nervous about my dashing, youthful good looks being altered. I needn't have worried.

Into the pulsating maelstrom of the gymnasium, with shouts and screams all around me, I stepped through the ropes and saw my opponent. He had hair he apparently called 'strawberry blonde', which could only be justified should strawberries actually be the colour of ginger biscuits. Behind his anaemic face I saw a fear worse than my own. Did he volunteer for this or was he pushed? It was looking, at this moment of truth, like he'd made a terrible mistake; as if he had entered a game of Russian roulette not really knowing the rules until sat at the table. How could I lose? Cheers went up as our names were called and the troops' numbers were chanted by opposing recruits.

The bell rang, its metallic echo drowned in a sea of screaming cheers. In I launched, jabbing quickly, trying to drive the freckles into his soft face. Nothing came back as

I ploughed forward, jabbing again and again, my left cross hitting him square on the jaw. He turned his back as if not wanting to play.

'Stop!' The referee stepped in. He turned my opponent back around as if he was in the trenches, telling him which way to go over the top. 'Box!'

On the order I pummelled him again; his nose splattered, red spray smeared across his rosy cheeks like a toddler with a ketchup bottle until the ref realised it was going to end in a mess. He stepped in between us to stop the fight.

Was boxing this easy? Having my arm held aloft in victory, I felt like a world heavyweight champion, not the victor in CTC's only light welterweight junior division bout. For the first time in training, members of my troop took an interest in me, shaking my hand, rubbing my head and congratulating my efforts to forge the reputation of 299 Troop.

I now felt regarded as an integral part of the troop. My jovial personality had made me popular in some quarters, but my slowness in taking up the skills of a good soldier meant some didn't particularly warm to me. People are often liked due to their abilities, not necessarily their character, and I fell part-victim to this. Possibly this is why wayward sports stars are supported through thick and thin. No matter what depths their behaviour sinks to, there are excuses to cover them. They may be a wanker of the highest order, but as long as they perform well on the field for the baying public then all is forgiven.

My boxing career – all one minute of it – had given me a newfound confidence and I even managed to go a day without a bollocking, something I'd targeted as a measure of success. I fell into bed listening to my Walkman, as I always did, too tired to get beyond the first song but with a smile on my face.

The next step in my ring career would take me to represent CTC in the Royal Marines Boxing Championship. The competition coincided with week eleven and 299 Troop's survival exercise: a week of living off the land with nothing more than a set of overalls and a tobacco tin of items that would hopefully keep us alive. Because of the importance of the boxing competition, I was informed that I was not to go on the exercise but to represent CTC instead.

On the morning of the competition, I skipped breakfast to ensure I'd make the weight. The boxers would be given a late breakfast after the weigh-in, where I could eat as much as I wanted and not get my knuckles wrapped by the chef for taking more than one sausage. The rest of the lads in the troop didn't know when their next meal would be, so they trotted off intent on gorging until fit to burst. They wished me well in the competition before I had to leave for the pre-weigh-in.

As we couldn't be considered a true team, not having trained together, the two PTIs allocated as our coaches needed us all to have a pre-weigh-in to ensure we could make the official weight an hour or two later. I was 61.1kg, well under.

'You need to lose 1.1 kilos, Lofty,' said the PTI with his clipboard. 'We have dropped you down to lightweight. We have a light welter already.'

This actually raised my confidence. The guys who I'd be up against would be smaller. There was just a small problem of losing that kilogram.

'You had a shit this morning?' asked the PTI.

'Yes, Corporal.' I wasn't lying.

'Go have another one.'

Off I trundled, taking my empty bowel with me, to sit on the toilet using colonic peristalsis to squeeze out something an accomplished tracker would identify as a pygmy spoor. I returned a little lightheaded and jumped back on the weighing scales. It seemed that my shit must have weighed 100g. It wasn't quite enough. I was thrown a bin bag and a skipping rope.

'Right, get in the sauna, put this bag on and skip for ten minutes. That should get rid of a kilo.'

I daren't tell him that I couldn't skip, so I entered the sauna in a black bin liner and jogged on the spot. I don't know how he thought I could skip in there, it was full of blokes in bin liners.

I finally came out feeling extremely lightheaded. Sitting in there was far worse than squeezing out a poo straight from the duodenum.

'Feeling okay?' said the PTI.

'Just a bit dizzy, Corporal.' I certainly felt fresh with the cold air on my wet face.

'Yeah, that'll be not eating and skipping in the sauna. Once you've had breakfast and rehydrated, you'll feel okay.'

At the official weigh-in I was terrified and visibly shaking.

'You got Parkinson's disease?' asked the PTI.

'It's not Michael Parkinson's disease, I haven't heard him say fuck all this morning,' added the other PTI who, up to now, had been with the bigger guys.

While I represented CTC along with the other recruits, not knowing each other only increased my feeling of loneliness. I looked around at the commando unit teams that sat in groups. Just the thought of fighting somebody from Zulu Company 45 Commando, even in my lighter weight category, put the fear of God into me.

Recognising this, the PTI who took me under his wing tried to compose me by saying my opponent would be just a normal bloke. Yeah, the sort of bloke I looked up to. In my mind, he would, by default, be a hard bastard who knew how to box. He wore the green beret, a commando boxer. I was a spotty little twerp who still owned a Subbuteo set. They must have looked over and thought I was the CTC mascot brought along to present a match-day coin.

Despite not having any breakfast and again evacuating my bowels, I was now in dire need of a nervous shite. On instruction, I approached the processing team to hand over my boxing card. I stood there pathetically, a Nigel of manliness.

'Junior Marine Time?'

'Yes, Sir.' Although I didn't know his rank, calling him sir was a safe option.

'It's "Sergeant", I work for a living.'

'Sorry, Sergeant.'

'It says here you're not yet seventeen. Is this correct?'

'Uh yes, Sergeant. I'm sixteen and three quarters, Sergeant.' It was as if I was writing a letter to *Jim'll Fix It*.

He called over my PTI. It was the first time I had heard a PTI called by name, not rank, a strange feeling – like knowing the first name of your primary school teacher.

'Al, you know this lad can't box.'

*That's a bit harsh*, I thought; *you've not even seen me.*

'He's too young.'

The PTI looked at me and then at the card.

'Time, you knobber, why didn't you say?'

Why didn't I say I was a junior marine? Why didn't I say I was sixteen? Why didn't I say I was too young? Probably because I didn't fucking know it mattered! Like everything as a recruit, I was just told to get on with it and not ask questions.

The sergeant turned back to me and returned the card. 'You better fuck off back to your troop then, Lofty, you aren't boxing today.' My PTI gave me a concurring look.

'My troop is going on survival ex today, Corporal.'

'Well, you better double back smartish then,' he laughed.

So double back smartish I did. The troop was parading in front of the accommodation block with that look of contentment only being full of beans and sausage can give. The troop sergeant laughed at my explanation of why I'd returned, ordering me to change quickly into the overalls I'd been issued for the exercise and bring my survival tin. I was going on a survival exercise with no breakfast or liquids, and just for good measure, a dehydrating session in the sauna for morning exertion.

If this wasn't bad enough, the insertion yomp was seventeen miles over the wilds of Exmoor, a task in itself even on a full stomach of energy-rich fats. On an empty stomach and the hydration of a thirsty camel with a floppy hump, the miles passed with only food in my thoughts and weakness draining my body.

The welcome finish line of the insertion march was a wooded glade that sloped down to a picturesque, babbling brook. At first glance it could have been the subject of a Constable painting, but this was not the time to admire the view. The sweat from our yomp would condense on our bodies and, in the cold of Exmoor, being without shelter and warmth could bring on hypothermia.

As we had been taught, we immediately searched for materials to make our shelter. Logs, brushwood and tin sheeting were all conveniently laid around the area; nevertheless, we had to first arrange these materials into some form to protect us from the elements. Being hungry and tired, the logs seemed heavier, the tin sheeting seemed to drag in the dirt and the brushwood wouldn't stay together as it should, but we continued until our first creation was complete. It had a roof and three enclosed sides, and under the circumstances it was bloody lovely.

Next, we searched for kindling and materials for the fire. Shelter was imperative, but warmth was another important factor in surviving the elements. By the time darkness fell, we had both. The yellow, flickering flames seemed to mesmerise us into primordial contentment. Sleep came easily despite the bone-aching cold; the cuddling of fellow men doesn't seem quite so odd when you have little more than a brushwood floor for insulation.

The rest of the week was spent being famished, foraging for kindling, setting and resetting traps that entrapped no prey but gave up plenty of stories of the one that got away. Even the plants and shrubs we'd been shown that were edible, if not nutritious, were only evident by their scarcity. Our group did manage to catch a few frogs, which didn't go a long way between the six of us, but a little frog was better than none.

We had been warned previously not to go scrounging from the locals, as some were pretty unhappy about our use of the area – especially as a previous troop had managed to hunt down, butcher and eat a sheep; it was all very commando-like but sheep rustling didn't endear us to the farmers. Yet the resourcefulness of the commando spirit lived within, so on the third day of hunger I decided to make a break for it and venture into the windswept desolation of Exmoor to scavenge from the local populace.

Despite being searched thoroughly by the training team prior to setting off on our insertion march, many of the troop had managed to secrete the odd £5 note on (or up) their person and we were allowed to bring 10p for use of a payphone in an emergency. As I didn't think I was going on the exercise I hadn't secreted anything, so I volunteered to go instead of paying into the communal fund, hoping the coinage given hadn't been shoved up anyone's anus, but being dark it didn't really matter either way.

Armed with nothing more than a shit-free £5.50 and a button compass with a permanently spinning needle, I left the shelter area and followed the fence lines towards the far-away lights of the Exmoor farms. Being a cold, clear night, reference-point navigation was pretty easy so I managed to get to the first farmhouse within an hour. After I knocked on her door, the farmer's wife looked at me pitifully. I must have looked and smelled like a Dickensian orphan, so she benevolently acquiesced to my request for any food she had to spare. Whether she had a golden goose I don't know, but she charged me £2 for six eggs. (If there had been a Tesco's nearby I could have bought six for 50p.) Unfortunately I was in the middle of Exmoor, so I suppose it only reasonable to pay a remote egg tax.

In her defence, the farmer's wife did throw in six slices of bread, but couldn't spare the wrapper so I had to accept them in my grubby, unwashed hands. Managing to secure an opened tin of beans from another farm, my shopping trip was complete. So began the four-mile return journey to the shelter area, trying to make sure that I spilled no beans, the eggs in my pocket weren't crushed and the bread I carried didn't soak up too much grimy hand sweat.

Greeted like the returning Messiah, I produced my wares to the group, hoping the darkness of the woods would hide the grubbiness of the bread. We boiled the eggs in the tin of water over the fire and quietly feasted on a meal fit for a tramp. Having buried the tin and eggshells, we knew we'd got one over on the training team and spent the next day gloating on our subterfuge. It's amazing how a little food will give you a spring in your step when hunger takes over, and our happiness was seized upon by the other recruits.

They say imitation is the best form of flattery. One of the other groups decided to have a wander the following night but, unfortunately, their mission ended after about 40m, snared by the training team. The training team was unimpressed, not necessarily by how the group had gone against orders but that they had been caught so easily. This was only going to end in unreasonable amounts of distress. We found out just how much the next morning.

The river in which we had attempted to catch fish became our aqueous gymnasium, as we thrashed out naked press-ups, burpees and sit-ups in the icy waters. Even worse, the guys who had been caught were doing the same exercises in their overalls. At least we could dry out naked in front of our fires and afterwards put on our dry clothing. For those poor guilty bastards, extreme cold, saturated clothing and continual shivering meant a real survival threat, one that was monitored by us as their mates and from afar by the sadists in the training team, to prevent paperwork.

As a reward for our gracious acceptance of a beasting, we were given pets. A rabbit was handed to each pair of recruits. We were instructed to give it a name and keep it safe and secure overnight. We knew what the outcome for the rabbit would be, but still we cherished its company. My oppo Stevie and I named ours Gordon, for no other reason than it sounded a grand name for a white rabbit; I am still hard pushed to think of anything grander. Cuddling it for twenty-four hours not only kept us warm, it also kept it secure in our possession. Some guys put theirs on a leash, using a snare as its collar before realising it was strangling the poor thing to a slow death; being cruel to the rabbits was something the training team would not tolerate.

The next morning, our leporid-loving training team brought us to a table where, placed upon it, was a rabbit similar to the ones we now held affectionately. After the normal introduction, the rabbit that had moments earlier been nibbling peacefully on a piece of lettuce was dead, blood dripping from its nose, its neck broken from a sharp chop by the corporal giving the lecture. Whether it was subconscious or not, I averted my rabbit's gaze; I didn't want it to see its brother executed.

For many recruits this was the first time they would kill an animal. I was 'lucky'; I killed my first rabbit when I was around seven years old. My grandad was a poacher, and our kitchen would be forever filled with skinned rabbits hung on a washing line, emanating that deeply appetising aroma of blood. After his poaching days were over, my grandad built a pen and filled it with rabbits. I would treat them all as pets and gladly feed them until they were as fat as Grandad liked. I don't know whether there was a hole in the pen but every so often one would 'escape', coincidentally on the day that we had 'boiled beef' pie for tea.

While harsh on the rabbits, the skills learnt were invaluable and had to take priority over any juvenile love of animals. My oppo for this exercise, Stevie, had never killed before, so he was keen to do the deed and I was only too happy for him to chalk up the first rabbit silhouette on his headboard. Nervously, Stevie held Gordon as instructed and chopped down hard on the back of his neck; the dull thud and whelp was echoed all around, as the mass chopping of bunny necks was sickeningly orchestrated like the soundtrack to an 18-rated version of *Watership Down*.

Gordon lay limp, but blood did not run from his nose. I was not convinced that Gordon was done for. Indeed, when Stevie walked away with Gordon draped over his shoulder the rabbit winked at me, just the one eye as if to say, 'Alright mate?' Was he trying to haunt me?

'Stevie, that rabbit's still alive,' I said.

'Nah mate, it's dead as a dead thing.'

'Well if it is, then it's the star of *Poltergeist IV: Rabbit's Revenge*.'

'Nah, it's the nerves still working.'

'I'd be fucking nervous if I was alive and draped over your shoulder. I'm telling you it's alive!'

As if to prove my point, Gordon started to thrash around violently. I don't care how many nerves it has, a dead animal cannot attempt to scramble over the shoulder of its attempted killer. I had to give credit to Gordon, he was a fighter, but my admiration for him was short lived. I snapped his neck with, it has to be said, a respectful remorse. Remorse over, Gordon tasted wonderful and his pelt made a smashing hat.

# EIGHT

*'My great concern is not whether you have failed,
but whether you are content with your failure.'*
ABRAHAM LINCOLN, SIXTEENTH PRESIDENT OF THE UNITED STATES
OF AMERICA

BEFORE PROGRESSING INTO the second fifteen weeks of training, we would first have to successfully complete a number of criteria tests. Fail anything and we would be back trooped. No pressure there then...

Firstly, we completed our PT pass-out. Although my feet were in bits, running around in pusser's pumps presented little problem and gym work was my strong point. The pass-out was a doddle, so too our Annual Personal Weapons Test (APWT) on the blunderbuss that is the now obsolete SLR and the even more archaic Sterling submachine gun (SMG), which was only useful in the hands of a *Star Wars* Imperial Storm Trooper – even if they did always forget to attach the magazine.

Thankfully, despite my slow start on the SLR, my shooting was actually quite good, achieving 119 out of 130 and gaining marksman status that entitled me to wear a crossed weapons badge on my dress uniform, which would be ridiculed by anyone from a commando unit. As with everyone else, my SMG test was successfully completed first time – not that I would ever get to hold one again.

Exercise Baptist Run was our last and most important test to assess our military skills thus far. I commenced the exercise with my feet in such a bad state that they felt like they'd been put through a bacon slicer.

Other than piss, the tried and tested way of preventing blisters was to use zinc oxide adhesive tape. Once blisters had formed the tape became an irrelevance, only pulling off the skin it was wrapped over. In my stupidity I'd persistently wrapped my raw feet in zinc oxide, meaning that every time I changed the tape I stripped my feet again down to the raw flesh. The balls of my feet looked like I'd stepped in boiling water and my heels should have been used on the set of a horror film.

Even setting off onto the exercise, I was in agony. The yomp up to Woodbury Common, although done many times already, was excruciatingly painful and I struggled to keep up, even at the relatively slow pace.

To assess our competency in soldiering, we would be instructed to navigate our way to a stance where a military subject would be tested. Most of the lads would rock up with that typical hangdog look of someone too tired to actually hold an expression. But not me, I impressed the training team. As I approached most of the stances they asked why I was smiling so much. But I wasn't smiling – I was grimacing in pain from walking on the raw flesh that masqueraded as my feet. The upside was that the pain overrode any nervousness I may have had in completing the tests. Yet getting to the tests was becoming more of a problem.

Fellow recruit Vince, an older cockney who was the agony uncle for us young lads, suggested I ask the training team if I could forsake walking between areas and get a lift. A well-meaning suggestion met a violent outburst of anger from the troop sergeant when I asked if this was possible. It was fair enough; the movement between each test was part of the test itself, although I thought him calling me a 'spineless piece of shit' a little unnecessary.

In retrospect, my childlike naivety can't have endeared me to the training team. But I was sixteen and stupid. As the exercise went on, so my confidence slumped with my shoulders as I struggled from one test to another, often late. When it came to the speed march back to CTC, I fell back within the first half-mile. I wasn't exhausted; I just gave up. I had, in Royal Marine speak, 'wrapped my tits in'. The pain was just too much to tolerate.

Even when we want something so badly, the pain doesn't subside. Our bodies still ache and our legs still don't work in the way we wish they would. I couldn't run another metre, despite having a green beret waved in front of my eyes and such encouraging words from the training team as:

'If you drop back any more, you lazy fucker, you've failed.'

'You're a waste of space, Time.'

And the classic 'Say goodbye to the troop, you spastic.'

On my return to CTC, arriving way after the rest of the troop, Exercise Baptist Run was finished. So too was I.

I showered quickly and immediately reported sick to get my feet sorted. In the sickbay examination room, the medics tore off the zinc oxide tape with unnecessary zeal and laughed at what they described as the worst pair of feet they'd seen in ages. The only applicable treatment now was to be covered in the dreaded iodine spray that would sterilise and protect them. Having knitting needles gouge out my eyes would have been preferable to the spray that disseminated pain so excruciating that even someone as eloquent as Stephen Fry would fail to convey the agony without adding 'fuck my old boots that hurts.' My inner mechanism laughed in agony, tears filled my eyes as I bit the pillow as if some sweaty man was trying to take my virginity.

'Hurts, doesn't it?' said the smiling medic who had a BSc majoring in sadism and minoring in stating the bleeding obvious.

I limped pathetically back to the accommodation in my flip-flops, dog-eared and downhearted. Corporal Stevens passed me with his normal sprightly gait; he looked like he'd just walked from a successful job interview, not from a week in the field.

'Time, you scrote, where have you been?'

I showed him my bandaged feet, hoping to elicit some form of sympathy.

'Soft cunt,' he sniggered, before walking off with the air of a man who had not a care in the world.

That afternoon we paraded to be told of the results of the exercise. The troop officer stood in front of us all, lined up in three perfect ranks. It wasn't often we saw him so his address was obviously important.

'There are some of you today who have not made the required standard we expect of you at this stage of training. It is not the end for you guys, but it is the end for you in this troop. It is up to you now to go away and learn again. Think of it not as failure, but as a deferment. It is up to you now to dig deep and go forward. However, if you don't think you are able to meet the required standards, now is probably a good time to have a word with yourself.' Names were called:

'Davies.' That was obvious, he was always in the shit.

'Haines.' His navigation was terrible. It was a wonder how he made it to the toilet without shitting his pants.

'Trickett.' Another biff, another weak link.

I hoped my name wasn't going to be called. But as is often the case in life, hope was just a denial of reality.

'Time.'

A part of my soul died immediately. Inwardly I knew I'd failed, but the confirmation destroyed me. Other names were called but I didn't hear them under the heavy, shoulder-depressing weight of disappointment. The gasps of relief and muted cheers made me sick to my stomach.

'To those of you who have passed, I pass on my congratulations. What I need you to do now is change into civvies, get your kit together and get ready for a week of adventure training in the sunshine of Cornwall,' he said, trying to calm down the celebrants before continuing. 'For those of you who have failed, you can clear out your lockers. You are no longer part of 299 Troop.'

That last sentence crushed me: my brotherhood since day one, my people, my troop, my mates.

The troop officer continued, 'Report to the CSM [company sergeant major], he will tell you your futures.'

With my heart dragging across the sparkling linoleum floor, I returned to my room. Sitting down, I stared at nothing, numbed to the bone. My world had collapsed. I was no longer part of 299 Troop.

I had never failed anything in my life that I really wanted to do. Sure, I'd failed chemistry at school but that was pretty much expected as I'd skived two years of lessons, in which the clueless chemistry teacher thought I was, quote, 'very quiet'.

But here I was, with my only goal in life to be a Royal Marines Commando and I'd fallen at the first real hurdle. How was I to continue? I was no longer an 'original'. I was to become one of those back troopers that would be mocked and looked down upon as an oxygen thief, especially as I'd failed Baptist Run.

The lads who I'd shared a room with for the past four months were too busy to offer their condolences. They knew I was weak, so it was of no consequence to them. I wasn't close to any of them so my anger turned to withdrawal. I packed in silence, my shaking body the only clue that I was frustrated, angry and trying not to burst into tears.

With my kit packed and my motivation thrown into the Exe estuary, I was among the eight failures the CSM brought into his office. I stood like a naughty child in front of the headmaster.

'Men, I can see you're all pissed off.' His powers of observation were outstanding. 'But your journey isn't over. It has just had a slight, how can I put it, interruption.'

I didn't really care what he had to say. It was alright for him, he hadn't failed.

'It's time for you to regroup, and get back on the horse. You now have to prove, both to us and to yourselves, that you are capable of passing not only Baptist Run but the rest of training.'

*Yeah, cheers for that. Tell me something I don't know.*

'I am confident you can all do that. I look forward to seeing you now putting this disappointment behind you to show everyone you are capable of becoming Royal Marines.'

As his speech became more encouraging my responsiveness waned further. The training team had always used a 'select out' method rather than the more modern 'train in' approach that the CSM was now offering. Encouraging and consoling words had, up until that point, been alien to us; words that now made the others seemingly feel slightly better about being abject failures. As for me, all I could hear was, *'You are no longer part of 299 Troop.'*

'He's right, you know, we need to get a grip and make sure we don't fuck up again,' said Davies, as we were dismissed to the NAAFI. 'I'm gonna smash it next time.'

'Yeah, me too, I reckon I only fucked up on my nav,' said Haines, to no one's surprise.

'Yeah, it must be all those shit compasses they keep giving you,' replied Davies to a ripple of laughs.

I remained quiet, distant from their renewed aspirations. I was still devastated by the first taste of failure. I rolled the CSM's words repeatedly around my head to salvage a modicum of inspiration. Yet his positive reinforcement seemed hollow. *'You are no longer part of 299 Troop.'*

'Nah, it's all bollocks,' I stated huffily to the group, now so positive it was a wonder they all weren't hugging. 'A failure is a failure. You can tell a duck it's a swan but at the end of the day it's still a duck.'

The once-smiling group now stood stern and silent. 'Quack,' announced Davies.

My grimace probably showed I was the only one currently lacking cheerfulness in the face of adversity.

\* \* \*

Before being placed into the troop directly behind us to retake Exercise Baptist Run, we would do some remedial military training with a trial 'Gibraltar Troop', specially set up for us numpties who couldn't get it right the first time.

A group of eight marching around camp suggested a number of things to me: we were on crabby recruit routine, we were on the way to the VD clinic, or we were failures that everyone would look upon with disgust and disdain. The fact that ninety-nine per cent of those on camp didn't know who we were, or didn't give a flying fuck, didn't register with me. My confidence crumbled by the day. By the time I had reached my new troop I didn't want to be there.

On the first morning in my new room, shared with five strangers I was convinced all looked at me with utter disgust, I decided not to stand when the DL walked in, as was protocol.

He stared at me, quizzically at first. 'Why the fuck are you not stood to attention, cunty bollocks?'

I got up lazily and stood there in a pose that very deliberately said, *Fuck off. Not interested.*

To his credit, he read it quite well. As a confirmatory

response, he stuck his pace stick so far up my nose that my nostrils were in my eye line.

'I have known hundreds like you, surly fucking twats who think they don't need to stand up when I walk into the room. They all ended up failures as well. Now get your fucking heels together before I take you around the back and fill you in, you cheeky little cunt.'

Appreciative of his fortune-telling abilities, I blurted out with a highly nasal twang, as his pace stick nipped my septum like a peg, 'I don't care, I'm opting out.'

There, I had said it. Opting out was the opportunity to leave before week twelve. I was in week thirteen but discretion was allowed for those who wanted to leave after this cut-off point. It had never occurred to me to opt out before, but here I was spitting it out to a man I'd met only ten seconds ago.

'Good. I'm glad you're giving up. The Corps doesn't need wrap-hands like you. However, between now and the time you fuck off you are still mine. Now I won't tell you again: get your fucking heels together.'

In the end, my nose situation forced my heels into surrender.

It seemed the altercation with my new DL had filtered through to my new section commander, Corporal Nash. The weapon-training stances, where I was going over the characteristics of a GPMG, became yet another hunting ground for members of the training team to test my resolve.

'Right men, we have a back trooper. Do we like back troopers?' It was his way of bringing his section even closer, a fortress that did not welcome outsiders even if they wore the same cap badge.

'No, Corporal,' returned the chorus, a little too like

American Marines for my taste. These lads I already disliked. We had not got off to the best of starts in the accommodation, with little in the way of a welcome. It was as if I tainted the bloodline of the troop.

'Apparently he's going to wrap his tits in today. Opt out. He can't hack it. Shall we give him a leaving present?'

I wasn't expecting a nice present with bows and a little message saying, *'Good luck, Mark ~ Love Cpl Nash and the lads xxx'*.

'Can we fill him in, Corporal?' asked one lad like a character out of *Lord of the Flies*.

Whether they could have was open to debate, but I couldn't be arsed to argue with these fuckers. 'Do your best then,' I said quite benignly.

As I had eight years before, when visiting my parents on their scummy estate, I laid down to await a kicking. Everyone stood around, not really sure what to do. One word from the corporal and they would have set upon me like wolves.

'Get up, you fucking lunatic,' ordered Corporal Nash.

I brushed myself down in a show of ambivalence, red with anger at my own uselessness.

'Right, fuck off to the troop sergeant. You're wasting my time. He can get fucking rid of you.'

I stormed away quickly, my boots crashing loudly into the gravel, glad I'd never have to see those twats again. It then occurred to me that I'd left my webbing in the weapon stance. I walked back, red with embarrassment.

'What the fuck do you want now?' asked Corporal Nash welcomingly.

'I've forgot my webbing, Corporal.'

'Fuck me, you'd forget your balls if they weren't in a bag. Go on, hurry up, you've taken up enough of my time.'

I rushed back into the weapon stance, ensuring I made no eye contact with any occupant. *Now* I wouldn't have to see them again.

I heard Corporal Nash start to talk again, masochistically hoping he was talking about me. However, he switched tone immediately as if distracted by swatting a fly. 'Right then, fellas, let's get this lesson started.'

By chance, my new troop sergeant was the Unsmiling Assassin from my previous troop. He had just been promoted and I was his first 'opt out' as a sergeant.

'You want to opt out? Why?'

''Cos I think I'm too young, Sergeant.'

'You got a job to go to?'

'Yes,' I lied.

He simply said, 'Okay, we will get you in front of the company commander this afternoon.'

That was it, as easy as that? Were they not going to try to keep me in? Was I so shit that they were completely happy to get rid of me?

Maybe they were right. Maybe I *was* really shit. I was too young to do this anyway. I should be out enjoying myself; not cleaning shitty toilets and parading around a drill square like some lobotomised monkey.

In front of the company commander, I saluted and requested to opt out due to not being mature enough to complete commando training.

'That may be true, Time,' replied the company commander.

'But many before you of the same age have had these same concerns and worries, yet have grown into men with extremely successful careers within the Corps. It would be a shame to see potential wasted by current immaturity.'

'I agree, Sir. But I still want to leave.' With stubbornness concreted into my soul, I was adamant.

As I was aged sixteen and still classed as a child, the company commander was obligated to my duty of care. Using his powers of discretion, he allowed me to opt out. I would be on a train home within forty-eight hours.

\* \* \*

What the fuck had just happened? At 07.30 that morning, I admittedly didn't want to be scrubbing a black toilet floor with a toothbrush and boot polish; but I hadn't ever thought of opting out before. I had just stated it in a spite of anger.

Sure, I was totally pissed off and hadn't handled my failure well. But opting out after all the effort I had put in? Here I was six hours later, booked onto a train to take me home. My career in the Royal Marines had lasted a whole fourteen weeks.

What was I going to do when I got home? I didn't even feel as if I had a home. Further education wasn't an option in October, and I was sure as hell not working in my mum and stepdad's fish and chip shop. I didn't want to end up smelling like a ginger girl's crotch.

I phoned my mum to tell of recent events and her response was one of mild indifference. My stepdad's was just as short.

It was up to me, but I had to get out and get a job when I returned.

My mind swirled, not accepting the events of the day. I once again cleared out my belongings to retreat to a sparse room for those who opted out, my own personal growlery. As the only occupant of a six-man room, I felt like the loneliest person in the world.

And for the first time since I could remember, I cried. I didn't cry when my gran died, but here I sobbed uncontrollably like the failure I'd become.

\* \* \*

The last full day of life in the Royal Marines was pretty easy. All I had to do was go through a leaving routine and hand back my kit and equipment.

Corporal Nash, the leader of the section I had gladly left, spotted me leaving my room.

'Oi, Time, get here.'

Even with my impending departure, I doubled toward him instinctively.

'So you are opting out?' he said.

'Yes, Corporal.' My heels were firmly together in attention.

'Why?'

'I'm too young, Corporal.' It was the truth. It was clear I was too immature for this commando life.

'Maybe so, but you will grow up. I was sixteen when I joined. Fucking tough, innit? I felt like opting out too. But you know what? If I had I wouldn't have had a clue what to do. Whatever it was it wouldn't have been half as much fun as being in the Corps. Stay in, son, and you'll get your rewards. But then again, if you think you can't hack it then leaving's probably the best thing, innit?'

He walked away, throwing the gleaming metaphorical gauntlet down at my feet.

I sat on my bed with a couple of other guys, opt-outs from different troops who had just arrived.

At this point, I would like to say that I vanquished the inner demons that strangled my will to continue by reading Sun Tzu's *The Art of War*, and the passage, 'He who knows when he can fight and when he cannot, will be victorious.' But I can't.

It was Peter Gabriel and Kate Bush, who were playing on Radio 1. Their song, 'Don't Give Up', had been played repeatedly over the last couple of weeks and now its words were all the more appropriate.

Music had always been a hugely important part of my life. If I hadn't let peer pressure affect me, I could have made it as a professional musician – although the career path of a flugelhorn and descant recorder prodigy is somewhat limited.

But songs had always stirred my soul, a motivational spur, a jab of remembrance, an emotional crutch. I listened intently, and realised that Peter and Kate were right. He hadn't been a regular feature in my music cassette collection, and her freaky-shrieky persona I wouldn't find arousing until a few years later; but together their words on this track smashed me into the realisation that I didn't want to leave.

I didn't really want to opt out, and my dark mood had been an uncontrolled vehemence lashing out at my failure. I wasn't yet ready to handle my emotions properly, and now I realised this I was better prepared to carry on.

The remedial training that I'd done in Gibraltar Troop had been of a high standard and the corporal teaching us had asked why I'd failed Baptist Run in the first place. It was because I had let my suffering feet overrule the rest of my mind and body. Now rested and healed, the break in training had allowed my battered and bruised body to recover enough to complete physical activity without feeling as though my feet were stripped down by forty-grit sand paper.

I requested to see the CSM, who passed on my request to carry on to the company commander. Twenty-four hours after being told I could leave, I stood again in his office.

'Back again, Time? You are taking up a lot of my busy schedule.'

'Sir, I would like to un-opt out.'

'I don't even think that is a word, Time, but carry on.'

'I have been thinking, Sir. I opted out because I was angry and didn't want to fail. I want to give it another go.'

'Okay, fair enough. Maybe you've grown up a little in this last twenty-four hours.'

Maybe he was correct.

'I will approve your request. However, you will have to give me an undertaking. From here on in you are to give it your best shot. Do you understand?'

It wasn't as though I'd regarded the experience like a Butlin's holiday up to now.

'Yes, Sir.'

'Unless you are not deemed suitable to carry on, or you

break your spine, you will not be allowed to opt out again. Is that clear?'

This seemed a fair deal to me, even if I preferred not to break my back. So with my well-practised gear-packing routine slick as a newly wet road, I was transferred to yet another troop.

\* \* \*

It's amazing what confidence can do for your wellbeing. My new troop seemed more accepting of me, and I shared my room with Charlie and Fred – a couple of fellow Yorkshiremen, and our homes were all within ten miles of each other. Fred was the original morale-in-a box on account of his strange usage of the English language, making us laugh with his absurdities that weren't even intentionally funny. I loved his ridiculous descriptive similes: 'as ugly as a carrot', 'as daft as a saucepan' and my all-time favourite, 'as gay as a bummer'.

Charlie too, was a star. He at once made me feel welcome even as a disgusting back trooper. A man of integrity, and immense generosity, he possessed a charm and smile that could turn the straightest man to consider the love that dare not speak its name...

Actually, no, that is going a little too far, but he was and still is a man who I look upon with genuine fondness. He would go on to have a hugely successful career, surpassing even my high expectations of him. We shared the same humour, same taste in beer, and we had both witnessed the legendary council-estate crumbly white dog shit.

The training team seemed as tough as most, but for some

reason less vindictive than my previous corporals. My new section corporal was even shorter than me. There always seemed to be an undertone of humour when he spoke, leaving me unsure whether to smile or just stare blankly. If he was being funny and I didn't smile, he'd suggest I didn't find him funny and give me press-ups. If I smiled thinking he was intentionally being funny and he wasn't, I'd get press-ups. In fact I did very well not to get press-ups whenever he spoke to me.

Exercise Baptist Run was repeated. Despite being a back trooper I was invited to share my bivvy with Fred.

'I don't want you to look like Barry No Mates,' he said.

'Don't you mean Billy?' I replied, appreciative of his skewed offer.

'No, I say Barry. It reminds me of Barry Manilow. He's not famous for having mates is he?'

And so this time, feeling like a confused audience member on a surreal TV show, I cavorted around Woodbury Common like a spring lamb, nailing the exercise, passing every test with flying colours. Finally, after much heartache, disappointment and cleaning, I had passed the first phase of training.

Our reward was a week's adventure training in the beauty of Cornwall's Penhale. Only a short drive from Newquay, it was where my first ever attempt at rock climbing took place.

When joining the Royal Marines on the first day, recruits receive a number of inoculations. One of those jabs is an anti-dancing serum. It doesn't matter whether the recruit is Billy Elliot's better dancing brother, the ability to combine commando operations with dance floor heroics becomes impossible, for it is written in the Royal Marines Commandments that thou shalt dance like a twat and so deliberately perform buffoonery in a night club to:

A. Prevent piss-taking by your mates;
B. Wind up civvies by bumping into them with chicken wings and ostrich legs;
C. Attract females who would otherwise just think you were trying to be smooth.

I certainly couldn't dance well. That is why at about 90ft, while climbing the cliff walls near Land's End, I was surprised by my fantastic Shakin' Stevens impression. Climbing can bring out the Shaky in all of us: limbs contorted at unnatural angles, strained muscles making alien movements, ensuring that when we're perched on a small lip the width of a wafer mint, our toes send a domino effect throughout our struggling body.

Some climbers call it the Michael Jackson leg, but I'd never seen Jacko quiver like the 1980s' Welsh rock 'n' roll star. It starts with discomfort in a toe. It shakes slowly. You try to stop it, only making it shake with ever more vigour, then it moves to your foot, then your heel, then your calf. Within ten seconds of the first toe quake it has rippled to your knee and you look like a naked Eskimo, unable to stop trembling.

Should you be conversant with such a dodgy predicament you can divest even more sympathy when I simultaneously suffered an excruciating attack of piles. Not having a proctologist's education, I don't know the technical term for a piles attack, but when those haemorrhoids play up it feels as though the devil himself has shoved a red hot poker up my sphincter. So for my

Emma Freuds to have a quick peek at the outside world just as I was a trembling wreck, perched on a rock face, was bad timing.

My screams were at first received with concern, but as I explained my predicament to my belaying partner, my new PTI, and the rest of the lads from my new troop, laughter replaced compassion. With the pain subsiding to a level where I could move, I scaled the last few metres like a sweaty spider monkey and tried to adopt a position on the summit where my chalfonts would withdraw to the safety and warmth of my back passage.

Through this sort of misadventure, I got to know my new comrades in a far more relaxed and civilised environment. In this atmosphere I actually caught one of the training team smiling, and not because he was watching us suffer.

\* \* \*

Reaching the fifteen-week mark allowed us to wallow in a job half-done. The Friday of week fifteen was Parents Day, an invitation to family members to come to CTC and see how their son/husband/boyfriend was coping and what he'd experienced in training so far. As we re-enacted physical training, weapon drills and fieldcraft skills to our highly impressed audience, for some reason we were no longer labelled 'scrotes', 'fuckwits' or 'oxygen thieves'.

But my parents were too busy frying chips to attend. So, along with Jock, the only other parentless recruit, we sat alone like a pair of cast-offs in the NAAFI bar, watching parents socialising with each other, sharing conversations of obvious hilarity with the recruits and the training team, who were wearing their civilised heads.

It was a case of 'what happens in Lympstone stays in Lympstone', as they clearly didn't want parents knowing that their little Johnny couldn't make a bed pack and had to swim for half an hour naked in the regain tank because he couldn't do a 'make safe' on his weapon quick enough.

The troop sergeant noted we were sat alone. 'Where's your folks, fellas?' he asked, downing a pint in the process.

'It's too far to come for mine, Sergeant,' replied Jock, whose parents lived in the far north of Scotland.

'What about you, Time?' he asked, sucking the beer head from his moustache. Before I could reply he interjected, 'They don't like you either?'

He could have had a point.

'Uh, too busy, Sergeant, they own a business.' I hoped I was making it sound as though they ran a multinational conglomerate and not a council-estate chippy.

'Right, seeing as though you are a pair of sad fucks you can thin out early on long weekend leave. Go on, fuck off.'

It was the most compassionate thing I had yet heard.

If my parents couldn't be bothered to come and see me, I took on the role of petulant teenager and decided I couldn't be bothered with them either. Heading straight to Knottingley, I spent the duration of the three-day weekend with my mates, not even telling my parents I was back. With my newfound reliance on my fellow recruits, mates had become my new family, and while the mates I went back to see weren't military they were still people I could rely on.

# NINE

*'If you think this is cold, wait 'til you get to Norway.'*

EVERY SINGLE BOOTNECK, WHETHER THEY HAVE BEEN TO NORWAY
OR NOT

WHEN NODS TALK about the second half of training, the general consensus is that as the intensity is cranked up the bullshit is lessened. What a load of bollocks...

On our return to CTC after a wonderful three days without getting flogged, we were greeted with a notice stating formal rounds of the accommodation were scheduled for 07.30 the following morning. Therefore, in between tales of numerous rejections from girls back home despite being a week sixteen recruit, those of us who had returned early cracked on with the familiar routine of cleaning every visible item, putting in extra effort to cover recruits who were returning as late as they possibly could.

No matter how much effort we put in, it was always going to be a waste of time. The training team, it seemed, was intent on making our return a difficult one. The standard of our accommodation was apparently way short of that nebulous mark of no tangible value.

After the mandatory flinging from the second-floor window of our bedding, the contents of our lockers were swept onto the floor in a rather childlike tantrum, leaving our room looking as though a Tasmanian devil had just visited. Fred muttered that the inspecting corporal was a 'cock muncher' as he stared out of the window at his clothing two floors below; yet even humour couldn't hide the fact we were being thrashed for no good reason. A lunchtime weapons inspection followed yet another room inspection. All these failed inspections apparently indicated we were still on leave and had to start switching on. These inspections would only get worse if they didn't get better.

Now, in Chatham Company phase two training, the training team needed to know we still had every bit of kit issued to us. The only way to do this was through us laying out a full kit muster, which was called after the evening meal.

Think of a kit muster as the desktop of a computer user diagnosed with obsessive compulsive disorder. Each item of clothing a computer file meticulously displayed in its rightful place in a certain way, in a certain position on the bed. Not only was the purpose of a kit muster to check our equipment, it was an easy way for the training team to pick us up should we lose any bits of kit or place an insufficient gap between items.

It was evident we were in the shit. The only variable was how deep. My kit muster now looked like the desktop of a deranged axe murderer. At 22.30 another kit muster ensued. I don't know whether they realised, but any kit we were now deficient in had probably blown away during their earlier hurling tantrums. Again, all our kit had to be laid out neatly on our immaculately-made beds. Every piece of equipment was scrutinised yet again, as if found on some archaeological dig. Anything that wasn't spankingly clean was thrown around the room. Nothing was good enough, unsurprisingly.

At 02.00 the DL woke us all and ordered us all out onto the landing. No shouting, no threats, just a quietly spoken order: 'Full kit muster, including beds, laid out on the bottom field, one hour. Go.'

It would have been suicide to suggest that it was raining and a kit muster in such conditions would only render it less useable for the next day. So, in the spirit of being fucked about for the sake of it, we rushed panic-stricken to our rooms to get all our beds and equipment down to the bottom field. Would it be better to arrange our kit muster on the beds now and carefully carry our beds to the field? Or should we get the beds there quickly and make shuttle runs back to the accommodation with our kit and equipment?

Fred and I took the former option. He was a good choice of partner as he'd been a removalist prior to joining up and so was expert at carrying large objects up and down stairs, a skill I doubt he'd ever thought would come in handy again.

We hurriedly laid out the muster before carrying the fully-laden bed carefully down two flights of right-angled stairs, out of double doors that were so heavy if one swung back it felt like you'd been punched by Marvin Hagler, down the steep stairwell to the bottom field, past the regain tank to plonk down the bed as neatly as one could expect on a muddy field next to the 6ft wall and tank trap of the assault course, all the while feeling the rain slowly drench our kit.

Watching others do the same, I could only wince as some got their angles wrong on the stairwell, their kit sliding from the bed onto the floor. This would cause a staircase bottleneck, with some cursing and those who saw the funny side of this whole exercise in bullshit giggling.

The DL returned to the accommodation block after half an hour to apologise. He hadn't realised it was raining so hard. He paused to gauge our expectant joy. The kit muster would now be under cover, in the drill shed. The bastard...

As word passed around the troop to those already neatly organising their clothes in the muddiness of the bottom field, the giggles turned to disquiet. Even Charlie, who up until now wore a permanent smile and would thank you for setting his head on fire, cursed in anger as once more we crash moved our beds to yet another location not designed for displaying beds.

At inspection time, the DL arrived. We all stood to attention. He, I am positive, revelled in the loathing of the thirty pairs of eyes now upon him. By now, we had all been taught a number of ways to kill someone. At this moment in time he was a likely candidate to be my first. He slowly walked around our beds, a cursory check here and a casual glance there. He occasionally commented with a big dose of sarcasm that our kit looked wet.

*No shit, Sherlock.*

But in the main, he walked around looking at our tired, angry faces. Then, without any further ado, he just plainly said, 'Good night, gentlemen.'

On the scale of 'good', tonight was well down. In fact it was pretty near the bottom. Although the kit muster was over, the night (or more correctly the morning) had just begun. Wiping our beds clean of mud, drying and pressing our wet clothing and equipment again, we had only another day of tiresome inspections to look forward to.

We were clearly under a 'welcome to Chatham Company' banner for the rest of the week, when constant beastings ended with the mantra that training would only get harder. We were certainly part of the teabag syndrome, which suggests the longer you are in hot water the stronger you become. We were on a rolling boil, under constant pressure from the moment we woke to the moment we crashed exhausted into our beds.

I occasionally bumped into guys from my original troop, and retold my stories of the continual beastings of week sixteen.

'Yeah, we did a full bed kit muster too, but in the River Exe, naked. You had it easy, geezer.'

Of course I should have known better. One-upmanship was prevalent in training and everyone had it harder than anyone else in the weeks behind them. This sort of black catting followed people through their careers. I am sure that, in 1664, when the forefathers of the Royal Marines were formed under the auspices of the Duke of York and Albany's Maritime

Regiment of Foot, number two troop got shit from number one troop about how their training was harder.

Yet the continual testing, including commando tests, is the benchmark. After beastings were discontinued in 2000, one could assume training had become easier, but as recent history has shown, in the last few years those guys have undertaken operations far more dangerous than I experienced, and performed with distinction whether they had to lay a kit muster in a field or not.

My contact with 299 Troop members also brought some quite strange news. Corporal Stevens, the man I'd admired with near hero-worship despite him throwing copious amounts of shit my way, had been killed in a road traffic accident. Apparently, he had inexplicably swerved in front of a lorry on the road up to Woodbury Common.

My shock and horror at this news soon subsided as the story continued. A new troop sergeant, evidently more sober than the man he replaced, had suspected Corporal Stevens was the infamous troop thief and had therefore set a trap.

Corporal Stevens took the bait and stole the £10 notes deliberately left there. It was him: a man who we looked up to no matter how much shit he gave us, a god, a bastion of honour and integrity, the sculptor who chiselled us into commandos, a King's Badge man, a sniper, a thief.

After all the shit I'd been given over the stealing accusation, and the humiliation it caused me within the troop, it seemed unbelievable that this man could watch it all go on around him and still continue to steal. He may have been initially revered by the nods, including myself, held in the highest regard around commando units, he may have even been a best mate to some; but to me, he was now nothing more than a cheap, cowardly thief.

*　*　*

While my physical fitness in the gym was of the highest order, placing a further quarter of my bodyweight onto my back added a whole new dimension to personal fitness. From week sixteen onwards, the bottom field was our new arena of pain.

The gym had been only the warm-up to the real challenges of the bottom field, the open-aired coliseum of the PTIs. The only things that could have made the bottom field more difficult were the addition of chariots and hungry tigers.

Our gleaming white tops, shorts and daps were replaced by denims, a PT top and a coat lovingly referred to as a 'beasting jacket', and our most comfortable boots. It would be here where the England Rugby Union team prepared for their successful 2003 World Cup campaign, and one would hope they received similar treatment in the glorious mud.

While I never failed anything down there in the chaos of battle fitness training (BFT), the high impact was taking a toll on my body. Conquering the high obstacle course, climbing 30ft ropes with the girth of an elephant's tadger, and a 90m fireman's carry in full battle gear carrying 70lbs of weight, two weapons, oh, and a fellow recruit, were the warm-ups to taking on the assault course: a well-chosen selection of obstacles placed in order to sap energy systematically from one part of the body to the next.

Already balls-achingly knackered, we would finish off in style: the full regain over the water tank, crawl along the chasm, a 15m rope stretched high above the regain water tank, halfway across slip the body around until it was inverted under the rope, release the feet from the rope, then swing them back on. From the inverted position, roll back over the top of the rope and continue onward.

The regain would have been easier if the rope across the chasm wasn't so slack. The bounce could make swinging a disaster should the momentum not be carried correctly. If the swing back onto the rope on the first attempt was unsuccessful, it was unlikely one could get back on without momentum. Should this happen, a series of ever more desperate yet comical, writhing air kicks, grunts, squeals and struggling would conclude with the PTI ordering the recruit to let go of the rope and fall into the icy waters of the regain tank, resurfacing to some earthy language.

Fortunately, I found the regains quite achievable, although I did fail once, making a pathetic splash – hardly pleasant in a British winter. As troops ran back from the bottom field it was always obvious who struggled on the regain rope, a troop of muddy but relatively dry recruits intermingling with a few who were saturated from their plunge.

In this second fifteen weeks it now seemed our CEFO (fighting order) – all 35lbs (16kg) plus weapon – had become an extension to our bodies. Apart from indoor lectures, we wore it everywhere during the working day. It felt like a goblin on my back poking and prodding me, making fun of my aching body every time I ran anywhere, banging into me to add more pain to the ever increasing webbing burns on my lower back that now took over from my blistered feet as the sores of choice. It was evident that the only thing more painful than running with webbing burns was showering with webbing burns.

Visits to Dartmoor became more frequent. Our night navigation exercises were longer, as our increasing familiarity with Woodbury Common meant the challenges it presented were lessened. Dartmoor, in national park terms, is the girl with the curl: when she is good she is very, very good, but when she is bad she is awful. When the sun shines across a blue sky, the moor is God's own country, the vistas across the tors, forestry blocks and dales truly enchanting. However, when the weather clags and precipitation is on the heavy side, it is a desolate, godforsaken place where no sane person would choose to venture. No wonder they put a prison there.

As Murphy's Law edicts, we only went there when it rained, snowed or the fog rolled in. I am sure someone at Okehampton Battle camp has a Dartmoor weather switch and whenever Royal Marines are scheduled to train, it's turned to 'cold, wet and miserable'. After all, we were often told, 'If it's not raining, it's not training.'

Venturing onto the moor for the first time filled me with trepidation. I recalled watching the 1939 version of *The Hound of the Baskervilles* with Basil Rathbone playing Sherlock Holmes. As a child it was only natural to be fearful of such a beast in grainy black and white, but my lasting impression was of the infamous, if fictitious, Great Grimpen mire – the bog that swallows the unwary.

The training team did nothing to dispel my fears. During winter these bogs were exceedingly dangerous; apparently they could easily swallow those who ventured too far into them. The prospect of dying a slow, sinking death in the middle of such a depressing place sent my overly imaginative mind into overdrive. Walking over wet, sodden terrain during the bleak nights that I crossed the moor became a frightening experience. Jumping from tussock to tussock was a good way to avert the 'quakers' and 'featherbed' areas of sodden earth, but the tussock jumping was a bone-shattering experience and ankles were easily turned.

The story goes that a young man was traipsing home across the moor when he came to a livid green 'featherbed'. To his astonishment, there in the middle of it was an expensive-looking top hat. Obviously, someone of the gentry had dropped it whilst trying to extricate himself from the mire. Never one to pass an opportunity, the lad delicately picked his way into the featherbed and picked up the hat. As he lifted it out of the quagmire his heart leapt into his mouth, for there, under the hat, was a human head. The sunken gent smiled and formally introduced himself in a posh city accent. The young man immediately started to heave the man out of the bog but, pull as he might, he could not budge him. Again, the gent smiled and explained that, if the lad would wait a moment, he would try to take his feet out of the stirrups of the horse he was sat upon.

We initially crossed the moors in 'syndicates', small teams to collectively navigate our way. As we grew more competent and our skills developed, we were dispatched on our own.

A dark Dartmoor night, with freezing fog wrapping around the body like a sinister cloak, scared the bejesus out of me. Regardless of my figmental fears, I cracked on with overcoming the real threat of deadly bogs, getting lost or not making the checkpoints in time.

It wasn't the usual location for someone celebrating their seventeenth birthday. The only cake would be the mud that dried on my clothing. It could have been worse though, I could have lost my compass jumping across one of the many small leats that criss-cross the moor.

It got worse.

Although I had always previously attached my compass to my lanyard, on this occasion I didn't. The only reason I can think of is that I was a dick. The leat wasn't all that wide, but as I leapt my wet boots gave way on the sodden, sloping bank opposite. Instinctively, I tried to grab some grass to arrest my fall, only to stupidly let go of my compass.

*Bollocks!*

I was soaking wet, alone, and on Dartmoor without a navigation aid.

*Happy fucking birthday!*

At the back of my mind was the fact that another charge was forthcoming. The compass was a starred item so it counted as equipment of value. And how the hell was I supposed to carry on without it? I could probably get to the next checkpoint using the reference points I'd pre-planned on my map, but that would mean an instant charge from the corporal at the checkpoint.

I was frantically hand-ploughing the grass, when along came

my knight in shining armour – or at least a heavy-breathing Fred in sweaty green combats, navigating the same route as me. Seeing my distress, like a true bootneck, after calling me a 'cock knocker' he forsook his own mission and assisted me in my search.

'Would it have fallen in the leat?' Fred asked.

It was arguably the most astute thing he had ever said, (other than when admiring the centerfold of a porn magazine: 'I can't see the point in her wearing shoes'). I accepted it was the likely whereabouts of my compass, but been loath to get into the leat in case it swallowed me like a bottomless bog. Now Fred was here he could pull me out if I did sink.

Stripped naked, at night on Dartmoor, I slowly lowered myself into the leat. I felt my feet grow numb as they sank into the freezing water and was slightly surprised when they hit the slimy bottom at knee height. Even more incredibly, my foot had trodden on something hard and metallic – my compass. My often-ridiculed monkey toes managed to pick it up. Naked, wet and cold on my birthday in the fog of Dartmoor, I couldn't have been more ecstatic.

Off Fred ran. 'Your toes could peel an orange inside some-one's pocket,' he shouted.

'Cheers mate, I love you too! Lots of beer in the NAAFI awaits you on our return!'

'None of that Southern shandy shit,' his voiced trailed as he continued into the darkness.

I sat alone once more, this time tying my compass to the lanyard, up to that point safely securing nothing more than fresh air in a pocket containing a half-eaten packet of biscuits and lots of fluff.

Instead of buying Fred a pint at the NAAFI, I decided I should at least attempt buy him a beer ashore. Nods going ashore wouldn't take their ID but would leave it in the guardroom in return for a personalised shore leave card, which did not have a date of birth on it. While this may have reduced the risk of ID cards being lost or stolen, to my criminal mind it raised the chances of getting served in a pub and allowed into Exeter's finest nightclub, Tens.

'Finest' may be a little optimistic. There may have been far better nightclubs in the town. I certainly hoped so, because Tens was one of those places where you would wipe your feet on the way out. Its clientele was clearly defined into three groups: women that wanted to go out with a Royal Marines recruit, local men who wanted to be a Royal Marines recruit, and Royal Marines recruits. It was no place for high fashion and champagne.

It sat below a pub named 'Winston's. Named after Churchill, I am sure the descendants of Britain's most revered leader of the twentieth century were overjoyed his name lived on through a pub. Winston's did serve its purpose, however, as the conduit between sobriety and the demise of mental faculties in Tens.

I was in a group of five recruits, including another birthday boy nicknamed 'Jim' due to his surname being Davidson. Nervous as I always was in entering a drinking establishment, I handed over my shore leave pass. The bouncer looked at it to confirm I was a nod, which was pretty obvious bearing in mind my haircut and limp.

'Keep out of trouble, lads,' said the bouncer, returning my card.

The smell of dry ice, Kouros aftershave and stale ale hit my nostrils, while Billy Idol's 'Rebel Yell' orchestrated the low-quality dance moves. I looked around keenly to see if there was any female that took my fancy. It may have been the fact that I'd looked at only men within the confines of CTC that made every woman look like Belinda Carlisle (this is 1986, remember).

I was still a virgin. Here I was trying to become a bootneck and I hadn't yet managed to get hold of a girl's left knocker. (I had felt a right one once. It was okay.)  Surely, here in this pit of debauchery, I couldn't fail to further my sexual repertoire?

'Happy birthday, short arse,' said Jim, holding a shorts glass in front of me.

'What is it?' I asked.

'Whisky.'

'I don't drink whisky. I had a bad session on it before I joined up.' It was true, if a little pathetic.

'And? Get it down you. I've bought it now.'

With the logic that my health and my wishes rated below the unnecessary splurge of a quid, I downed the whisky so as not to offend Jim. It was immediately obvious that this was a mistake.

With that familiar feeling welling up, using skills taught in the 'Why Things Are Seen' lectures, I quickly scanned and searched for the toilet sign. Excusing myself, I pushed quickly through the doors. That distinctive public loo smell of shit, sick and piss-soaked fag butts didn't lessen my need to puke; finding little in the way of open toilet stalls, I barfed my ring up so violently into the urinal that it splashed back onto my shirt and all over my shoes, much to the hilarity of a fellow nod pissing into the nearby sink.

'We've just bought Jim a death wet,' said Fred as I returned, teary-eyed, into the darkness. 'We were gonna buy you one but thought you might actually die.'

The 'death wet', or 'top shelf run' as it was otherwise called, was a pint of every available spirit on the top shelf, with a splash of either coke or lemonade added to reduce the risk of an appearance at the coroner's court. Jim stood at the bar, with his cock out for no other reason than that's what he liked doing. Taking the pint glass, he downed the death wet in one go. It was rather impressive (the drinking, not his cock, although it was certainly bigger than mine).

I stood with my pint of flat beer, not even sipping it for fear of another bout of vomiting, looking at anyone who would return my gaze.

Someone did. She was nice. Very nice in fact, far better than the girl I'd passed en route to the toilets, pissing in the corridor as she couldn't wait any longer.

She smiled at me. I smiled back. She smiled again. I again returned my smile. I must have looked like a simpleton. With the fuzz of alcohol giving me the required courage – as defined by the qualities of a commando – I approached her.

'Ayup,' I said in the poshest northern accent I could muster.

'Alright.' Her Devonian greeting made her sound like a pirate.

Silence ensued. That was it. I had failed to prepare any conversation beyond regional salutations. She could see my discomfort.

'What week you in?'

It wasn't the romantic opening gambit I'd expected. Okay, so I would have been fortunate for her to say, 'I saw you standing there and our body language suggested we had a mutual attraction, and my, you are a fine specimen of manliness.' But I wasn't expecting her to quiz me on my progress at CTC.

'Uh, week eighteen now.'

'You got Silent Night coming up week after next then.'

'Yeah.'

'Got your patrolling skills weighed off?'

I was confused. Was I talking to a girl or a Royal Marine dressed in women's clothing?

It was only at this point that I suffered a little paranoia, wondering if she could smell my vomit-tinged breath. Thankfully, before she could get another whiff, Fred butted in, grabbing me roughly around the neck.

'Ayup Doris, can I plait your hair with me feet?'

Even I could see Fred's drunken spittle hitting her.

'Smart bloke,' she replied, in a fashion rather too bootneck-esque for my liking, before she walked away to talk to another recruit.

'Fuck me, Fred, I was in there,' I lied.

'Yeah, 'course you were. Mate, stay away, she's been through more blokes than a dodgy curry. They call her "the Adjutant". She's been invited to nearly every passing-out parade.'

To be honest, at my level of sexual frustration I'd have quite happily had my balls fondled by the actual adjutant.

\* \* \*

The following morning I actually felt okay. I'd managed to purge myself of most of the alcohol through the medium of puke and had sensibly drunk a bellyful of water before sleeping. I rose from my bed and spotted a few dark splashes on the linoleum floor. Initially, I thought it was blood. But as my senses awoke, I could smell it. It was shit.

Seasoned animal hunters will often track 'scat' in their quest to find a prey. It is generally regarded as an advanced skill, with an understanding of animal habitat, a keen eye and a lust for vanquishing quarry as must-have qualities. But even a myopic vegan could have easily followed this particular trail of shit.

It led from the doorway to Jim Davidson's bed in the corner of our room. He was laid on top of his sheets naked, but for a forlornly hanging sock which had seemingly stepped on one of his own brown landmines. He was face down, luckily enough, because his face was also lying in a dried pool of vomit.

'What the fuck is that smell?' Fred had by now awoken.

Fred shook Jim, hoping he wasn't a stiff. In case they all smelled that bad, I made a mental note never to work in a mortuary.

'*Hnnh?*' Jim raised his creased head. Realisation then hit him. 'I think I've pissed the bed.'

'You think? I think you've done more than that,' replied Fred.

Jim looked down to see the overt display of his bodily fluids. 'Fuck,' he said, before allowing his head to fall back into his vomit to sleep off his hangover.

It was my first exposure to the Holy Grail of overindulgence, the 'grand slam'. I wasn't to know at the time, but it certainly wouldn't be my last.

The rest of us agreed we couldn't think of any better way to spend our Sunday morning than cleaning up our mate's shit trail. Utilising our newly acquired skill of judging distance through a unit average, it measured twelve metres. And there are people who say there are no civilian uses for military skills.

\* \* \*

Day by day, I felt as though I was getting to grips with the tasks and challenges set before me. I now even looked forward to more weapon training. I threw my first live grenade with gusto. I wanted to shout, 'Achtung pigdogs!' like in the war comics, but followed protocol and boringly shouted, 'Grenade!'. I learned about mortars, rocket launchers and machineguns, all pieces of equipment designed to inflict all manner of death. We learnt advanced patrolling tactics, feeling like a real soldier pretending to hunt down or ambush the enemy, so as to further inflict all manner of death. In fact, my portfolio of ways to inflict all manner of death was increasing by the day, and at seventeen it was frustrating that I wouldn't be able to legally inflict all manner of death until I was at least a year older.

Moral questions of killing had never arisen during training. Killing was in our job description and the various methodologies were didactically written in my innocent-looking red plastic ring binder, known as an affairs folder, just as an apprentice mechanic would describe the diagnostics check on a 1986 Mini Metro.

By now, those recruits who harboured any moral dilemma would have taken a one-way train trip from CTC. I never questioned whether these lessons were ethically right or wrong. The morality of killing was never broached formally and personally it was never an issue, due to my immaturity.

I had, though, progressed past the phase of joining up for 'Queen and country'. I was now doing this to protect my mates, a camouflaged, portable human shield with only the welfare of my colleagues at heart. How I would handle killing another human, only time would tell.

Week nineteen was Exercise Silent Night, topically leading us into the final week prior to Christmas leave. While shepherds watched their flocks (for fear of them being butchered by Royal Marines recruits) and snow lay on the ground all around, it was no Christmas carol. If I were to be eloquent, I could suggest that my joyful soul was numbed by the mournful cold. Or I could just say it was fucking freezing all bastard week.

Fatter people are often said to withstand the cold better, but before I nipped off to eat a bakery's allocation of pies, the bigger guys looked as cold as I did. None seemed overly comfortable in the conditions.

The training team had advised us that the conditions were to be 'wintry', and suggested that when in town we should invest in some long johns or, even better, tights. I bought both just to be on the safe side. (I would have liked to say it was my first time of wearing women's clothing, but I would wear my mum's knickers if I had no clean pants left. Thank God I was never run over.)

I never ended up wearing my long johns. The sheer feel of the light tan material sheathing my legs in a swaddling of 40 Denier ecstasy was enough to make me forget about baggy undergarments. But it was a pity I didn't venture into some lingerie shop to buy a full body stocking, as my top half was permanently frozen.

If feeling like a German sat on the outskirts of Stalingrad wasn't enough, on yet another crash move I walked into a tree. On a funny video show it may have looked hilarious. However, this tree, like many in the training area, had branches cut off to assist in the application of bivvy ropes and bungees, leaving sharp, peg-like stubs sticking from the trunk. When pitch black it would be feasible, if not unlucky, to walk into one of these, yet luck was not on my side. A stub poked me directly in the eye, knocking me to the ground in writhing agony.

'Who the fuck's that?' screamed the troop sergeant.

'Me, Sergeant!'

'Who the fuck is me?'

'Time, Sergeant.'

'Keep the fucking noise down, Time.'

'I've nearly poked my eye out, Sergeant.'

'Well, try harder next time and do it fucking quietly.'

It was quite alright for the training team to throw thunder-flashes and shout all manner of aggressiveness at us to expedite our crash move, but woe betide me for screaming when my eyeball was skewered onto a tree.

A magic eye pad was applied for the next couple of days. I say 'magic' because I was mystified as to how it worked.

Still in agony, I walked around looking like I'd returned from the Somme, intermittently treated by a visiting medic who squeezed some liquid into my eyeball in a successful attempt to make it even more painful.

My weapon had become my new best friend, especially on exercise, and was never too far from me. In fact, the designated acceptable distance anyone could be apart from their weapon was a 'hop, skip and a jump' away. Willie Banks was the triple jump record holder of the day with 17.97m. While I wasn't a 1.9 m tall Afro American athlete, I thought I could at least stand around 5 metres away. As per usual I was totally wrong. According to the training team, a hop, skip, and a jump constituted a distance of about 2ms - the world record for guinea pig triple jumpers, I would wager. I was punished not long after for offending against this rule, despite being virtually next to my weapon as I dug a shell scrape. Although with an eye patch I had lost a degree of depth perception, I was pretty sure I was within the prescribed distance. The troop sergeant was a sniper so he could accurately judge distance over hundreds of metres, but it was obvious his short-range measuring was in slight need of recalibration. Once again, non-tactical burpees overrode any inclination to argue my point.

When on exercise, one of the most reassuring thoughts was that upon return to camp we would have a nice, warm shower and a bed to curl up into. So, on the Thursday evening as we yomped back into CTC, our thoughts turned to scrubbing off the week's travails and getting a good night's kip before going home for Christmas.

The bastard training team had different ideas.

I assume they were environmental trailblazers and that turning off the accommodation's heating system was saving a panda somewhere. But given the choice between a hot shower after a week freezing my tits off or saving an endangered animal, I would happily piss on the frigid fat furry fucker's over-sized coffin if it meant getting the radiators turned on.

With no respite after exiting the shower, I wore my unused long johns to bed. For the first time since I'd been at CTC I covered my bed with a blanket, falling into an uncomfortable, shivering sleep. I was better off in the field.

We awoke early. It was Charlie who found a build-up of ice on the windowsill, where rivulets of condensation had frozen. He had been up most of the night, a shivering, gibbering wreck despite wearing all his layers, forsaking sleep to avoid dying of hypothermia.

Nods are now given duvets, which if anything makes recruit training harder. There is nothing worse than getting up from a comfortable bed when your breath is visible. As we only lay on board-hard mattresses covered in the most uncomfortable of sheets, getting out of bed was a welcome relief for us. Although getting picked up for having ice on the windows at our morning inspection was a little bizarre.

But we cared not a jot. They could give us as many press-ups as they wanted and call us any name they saw fit. By midday we would be going home for Christmas leave.

# TEN

'*Do you know what "nemesis" means? A righteous infliction of retribution mani-fested by an appropriate agent. Personified in this case by an 'orrible cunt... Me.*'

BRICK TOP, *SNATCH*

AS A POST-CHRISTMAS present, prior to weeks twenty-one and twenty-two and our live field firing exercises on Dartmoor, a new corporal joined us.

He addressed us in a thick Liverpudlian accent. 'I am Corporal Hagar, like in Hagar the Horrible.'

I thought, *He's a Scouser; he must be up for a laugh.*

'Hagar spelt B.A.S.T.A.R.D.'

*Maybe not then.*

A nervous laugh rippled through the troop.

'You won't be laughing tomorrow.'

As it turned out, he certainly wasn't a lying bastard.

His standards were of the highest order; so too were his punishments that were meted out for even the slightest misdemeanour.

He couldn't have joined at a worse time. January on Dartmoor was as cold as usual, very cold in fact. Snow had fallen more than in previous years and temperatures regularly fell below freezing.

On our first week of field firing, temperatures recorded were the lowest for the Southwest region in the whole of the twentieth century. Wrapping up warm would have been nice, but our wet combats didn't really do the trick. Running, diving, crawling through the sleet and snow of Dartmoor during section attacks entailed wet clothing from the first few minutes.

On day one, we practised our first dry attack – 'dry' as in no rounds fired; it was exceedingly wet underfoot and the permanent sleet made the conditions ideal for whimpering. Committed to the cause, I dived enthusiastically every time the order was given, ignoring the jolt my body suffered in hitting the frozen ground. After we finished what I thought was a textbook attack, the troop sergeant held aloft a magazine.

'Right, one of you has lost this. Check your pouches now.'

We all checked. My heart sank. *Fuck*.

'It's mine, Sergeant,' I shouted meekly, my raised hand now a beacon of ineptitude.

He threw the magazine to Corporal Hagar, who would decide my fate.

Along the side of the range was a stream. In the summer it

would be a nice accompaniment to gambolling lambs happily prancing along its bank. In January, it acted like an angry Scotsman (coincidentally like my troop sergeant).

It belted along, seething and swirling, swollen with rage. At the point where we stood stones had been moved, either by design or by nature, and had formed a small reservoir diverting from the main stream. Corporal Hagar imaginatively named this 'the jacuzzi'.

'Time, this magazine is dirty and I don't mean like *Razzle*. I reckon the best way of cleaning it,' he added, looking over to the jacuzzi, 'is a good wash.'

With those kind words of advice, he threw it in. 'How many magazines have you got?' he asked, his scouse accent as sharp as the surrounding ice.

'Three, Corporal.'

'How many should you have?'

'Four, Corporal.'

'Where's your other one?'

'In there, Corporal,' I said, pointing to the jacuzzi.

'Well, you better go and get it then.'

Off I ran, fully clothed complete with webbing, into the jacuzzi. I have to say it wasn't quite like the jacuzzis I'd heard about. Weren't they were used by nubile Scandinavian girls and wife-swapping Americans?

Only the fast-running stream stopped the water from icing over, yet the grass alongside, spray-painted with white frost, indicated to me that if it was cold getting in, I was going to be extremely cold getting out. I told the corporal in between gasps of lung-imploding coldness that I couldn't find my magazine.

'That's 'cos you're being weak. How are you going to find it like that? You've not even dunked your head under the water.'

Keen not to be labelled weak again I put my head under, my snotty face numbed even more. Even with my amazing sub-aqua skills, the magazine couldn't be located.

Out I got and for the next hour I seriously thought I was going to die. I'm sure the training team was checking me from afar for signs of hypothermia, even if Corporal Hagar was too busy throwing thunder-flashes at everyone in the hope it would warm them up, or set them on fire. That familiar feeling where the torment of cold is replaced by the contentment of warmth, as the first hot flow of coffee percolates through the body, ensured I survived the rest of the day.

After such a traumatically cold and exhausting day, it would have been nice to return to a hot bath and a warm bed, but no. Our accommodation was Standon Farm, a derelict farmhouse taken over by the MOD. It had previously gained infamy as it was purportedly where, in the 1960s, Secretary of State for War John Profumo took Christine Keeler for a bit of how's your father. Now the place looked like somewhere you would only take your mistress to murder her.

The farmhouse was pretty simple, but we weren't worthy of sleeping there. We were in the barn where animals had taken industrial action when asked to accept the conditions. We washed and shaved in the stream outside in the mornings and jumped into the stream after a day on the ranges.

Having nowhere to wash and dry our wet clothes, we would, on our return from the ranges, hang them in the drying room, though in January it was more of a damping room. After a stream (not steam) bath, I would towel dry quickly, rubbing over goose bumps the size of pimples. My hands tingled with cold as if dipped in battery acid and I wondered whether my lips were as blue as everyone else's. I would then change hurriedly into my one set of dry clothes. The warmth of wearing dry clothing was like being wrapped in an electric blanket. It was the highlight of the day. Even the hated haybox meals were greeted more warmly than the food itself.

As I'd been thrown voluntarily into the jacuzzi, my clothes from the previous day were still wet when I put them on for the next day of range work. Putting on cold, wet clothes after a warm night in a sleeping bag would now be deemed a human rights abuse in a European court. But that's what I willingly did, and so before the working day had even started I was piss-wet through and teeth-chatteringly cold.

As per usual, at the end of the range day we had to declare that we had no live or blank rounds in our possession, holding out our magazines for proof.

'Hmm, Time?' Corporal Hagar would ask.

'Yes, Corporal?'

'How many magazines do you have?' There was an obvious answer, staring right at him.

'Three, Corporal.'

And so again the theatre was repeated. Into the jacuzzi I'd jump with the same luckless result, reappearing from the cold froth without said magazine. This game lasted the whole of the first week. It didn't seem to get any less funny for the training team. Corporal Hagar had become Corporal Schadenfreude, the main architect of my misfortune, which filled him with unbridled glee.

It certainly didn't get any funnier for me. To take some heat off me – not that there was much heat in such conditions – another recruit lost his magazine. But as it was on the Friday he only had to leap into the jacuzzi once, and without calling the lad a wimp, he made a bit of a meal of it. I was honour bound to retake my role as the jacuzzi king and leapt with gay abandon back in, but still could not find my magazine. Although I did find his.

The troop sergeant commended my actions as 'strong' and so, while I was shivering to the bone, I'd at least proven myself to be game for anything. In recognition the troop sergeant gave me a spare magazine. It would have been nicer if he'd given me it on the Monday, but from thereon I never lost a magazine throughout my time in the Corps.

\* \* \*

The problem with range work on Dartmoor in January was that the inclement weather often reduced visibility to a degree where the range became dangerous and was deemed 'fouled'. All shooting stopped and the training team became bored, so after recounting our fuck-ups even beastings were repetitive and boring.

With a troop of thirty-odd recruits to play with, they had to find ingenious and comical ways of passing the day. Fred won the 'best wanking face' competition before the more skilful 'Special Olympics' were called, where the sports of bog hopping, range crawling and trench jumping were invented. Scotsman's piss-up was hilarious, where a nod ran in a shuttle sprint to one end and was spun round numerous times until deliriously dizzy, then sent back to run in whatever direction his disorientation took him, sometimes into the nearby stream.

Elsen sprints were a less popular sport for nods; we would be timed over a set distance carrying the portable toilet full of shit, piss and dangerous chemicals, hoping we didn't trip over the uneven, slippery surface. The Scotsman's piss-up was eventually combined with elsen sprints but ended abruptly when the first nod emptied the full elsen all over himself and the gravel road leading to the farm. It's extremely funny when it happens to someone else, believe me.

The haybox meals, usually consisting of stewed meat of dubious origin, would be accompanied by unlimited loaves of bread and far too many blocks of margarine. It was law that everything had to be eaten. Even the most ravenous could only willingly eat so much bread and margarine, but as the troop sergeant explained, 'You don't know when your next meal will be.'

In reality, it was highly likely to be around 18.00 that evening.

Nonetheless, all bread had to be consumed and impromptu dry-bread eating contests were called until all that was left was the margarine. If the galley staff had been in a benevolent mood we'd only have possibly half a block left, but if the chef had a hangover, or was a bastard, we'd have more blocks than necessary to spread on the bread. Raw marge does not appear on restaurant menus for a good reason. According to one of our corporals, the aim of forcing us to eat margarine was to create internal waterproofing to ensure none of us drowned. What a pile of shite...

What actually *was* a pile of shite was the mountain we made from sheep droppings. Corporal Hagar decided that, as the range was fouled again, we should create the original 'dirty bomb'. Diligently collecting droppings in our helmets, we dumped them into one huge pile that eventually grew to knee height. As we stood in a circle around the pile of shite like Pacific sailors watching a nuclear explosion, Corporal Hagar lit the Mk8 thunder-flash and pushed it deep within the mound.

'Don't any of you move a fucking inch,' he said as he hypocritically retreated away from the lit fuse.

The thunder-flash exploded. The dirty bomb was more Bobby Sands than Bikini Atoll, peppering us all in smouldering shit to the hilarity of the training team. We were already covered in plenty from crawling and diving along the moor, so a bit more shit, albeit in the facial region, wasn't going to harm us.

While the operating of an observation post (OP) was not necessarily in the curriculum, with time on our hands the training team decided extra military instruction would be more useful than making us run around doing elsen sprints. While we didn't have to lie for hours logging the movement of a dodgy-looking farmland animal or try to keep awake through the night, we did get taught the insertion, construction, administration and extraction of the OP. Bearing in mind we may have been stuck in one for days, if not weeks, the administration was important to ensure optimal efficiency.

The training team enlightened us by demonstrating the various actions required to ensure an OP ran smoothly.

There are many pamphlets out there that describe how to teach military skills. But I am struggling to find one entitled 'A Lesson on Shitting in a Plastic Bag'. We got one. I'd have quite happily taken theoretical instruction; after all, how hard can it be? But we got a physical demonstration by one of the corporals. It would have been nice if the troop sergeant had picked someone who was confident in his bowel movements, as the corporal who did the demo clearly wasn't.

'Get closer, in fellas, so you can see clearly how this is done,' he said to a less than enthusiastic audience.

Faeces, as any medical professional will tell you, actually has a classification scale called the Bristol Stool Scale and seven levels of firmness. Level one is where a stool is separated into small, hard nuggets that are difficult to pass. At the opposite end of the scale is level seven, where the stool is entirely liquid and where one could 'shit through the eye of a needle'.

The demonstration would have been far easier for all parties if his stools were at levels three to four – a cracked or smooth sausage with the consistency of marzipan. Unfortunately, he was either suffering from dysentery or had been on a diet of stout and kebabs for a year. Rather than plopping a sturdy turd into the bag, his anus sprayed level-seven brown bits around the area like a malfunctioning water hose, all to the hilarity and disgust of everyone captivated by this lesson in lunacy. In fairness, he did actually capture a small amount of shit in the plastic bag; however, the majority was anywhere but.

'As you can see, fellas,' he said after wiping his arse. 'Sharing an OP with someone who has the shits isn't ideal.'

We'd pretty much deduced that already.

On the Saturday morning, instead of watching *Football Focus* or bedding down to read the paper, like any normal person when there's a near-hurricane blowing up outside, we conducted a speed march over Dartmoor.

Although only four miles in length, the route was as horrendous as the weather. With horizontal rain stabbing the face, the route was ninety per cent uphill at a pace to test our resolve, causing my stumpy legs to swim in a riptide of lactic acid. The finish was a lap around the drill square at Okehampton Battle Camp.

I was amongst the shortest in the troop, so I was always at the front of the column at speed march time so I hadn't even had without the benefit of anyone shielding me from the weather. Halfway around the drill square, the troop sergeant caught my dwarf-like legs stuttering out of step just long enough to get me thrown to the back.

At the finish, a ghostly mist of sweat swirled into the cold air from our clothing as we stood to be addressed by Corporal Hagar. Out of the van came the lads who'd fallen behind, unable to keep up the pace.

'Time,' said Corporal Hagar, 'join those clowns from the wrap wagon.'

I looked at him quizzically, and remained on the spot. This was probably viewed as insubordination, so I was unceremoniously dragged over to the van that followed every speed march, the truck of shame known as the wrap wagon.

'You're a short arse, Time. That means you were supposed to be at the front. You ended up at the back. So you've failed.'

No, not the 'f' word, not failure again. I couldn't handle failure. My body lurched into disappointment and once more my confidence was shot. Fred and Charlie gathered around me, consoling me that the team had done it to test my willpower, just like throwing me into the jacuzzi every day.

From that moment I took a 'fuck you' attitude to the training team. If they wanted to play these silly games, let them. They wouldn't break me. My motivation had changed from proving to myself that I could pass out to proving the training team wrong.

*Fuck 'em.*

The next morning the failures did a rerun. If anything it was harder; maybe the training team wanted some of us to fail and so pushed up the intensity.

*Fuck 'em.*

With my breath shortening and my legs pounding, I wasn't going to let an inanimate object like a hill beat me. But it was. The hill seemed to get steeper and longer, the cold air rasping at the back of my throat as the pace gathered. My thighs screamed, lactic acid built up in my calves, my step scrambled out of time and I was warned by the troop sergeant to get back in or get in the wrap wagon.

As I thought the hill would never end, we came to its brow. I got my body sorted and found the famous second wind.

At the finish, the troop sergeant stood to our front. 'Four miles in under thirty minutes, that's not bad, considering the route,' he said, the green beret on his head collecting condensation. 'Be aware, that's the easiest speed march you will do from now on.'

Those words felt ominous.

Returning to CTC, struggling for confidence, the BFT pass-out was probably the tonic I needed to get 'back on the horse'. Royal Marines Physical training is a graduated and scientific programme designed to prepare us for the rigours of war. The Institute of Naval Medicine had conducted a study that suggested the need for a particular type of athlete. Runners usually don't have good upper-body strength and upper-body gymnasts aren't great at running. Royal Marines training sought to create endurance-based strength athletes, all-rounders with highly capable physiques. BFT training is an ideal method of achieving these aims.

While feeling extremely knackered after every BFT session, I found the bottom field a place where I could regain credibility. The PTI found me to be one of the stronger of the troop and, as a fellow Yorkshire man, liked the effort I put in.

Someone who didn't particularly like putting in the effort required (and as such, I'd imagine, suffered for it) was HRH Prince Edward. He decided he'd had enough, officially wrapping his well-groomed royal tits in. Not binned, or back trooped, or even convalescing through injury, he'd decided life as a wannabe commando officer was a bit too difficult.

It was brilliant. Although I'm sure the bureaucrats were disappointed that someone of such standing was leaving, and therefore no longer guarding against any future defence cuts, for us working-class buffoons, who saw the green beret as a challenge for only the deserving, his admission that training was beyond him propelled our elitism into the stratosphere.

Soon, new t-shirts were worn around camp stating, 'You can turn a frog into a prince but you can't turn a prince into a Royal Marine.' Unfortunately, they only were made in size medium and upwards.

The tabloids made a huge issue out of his resignation and press releases detailed how lonely he'd been; how he felt pressurised as a royal to do better than his peers; how he was brutalised by instructors with a loathing for academics. Of course, his C and D grades at 'A' levels and his lower second-class degree in history were clear signs of his superior intellect. As for feeling pressure, I think the term could be more accurately applied to those who struggle to put food in front of their children, or soldiers pinned down under enemy fire.

The next challenge, for those of us whose parents weren't the wealthiest land owners on the planet, was to survive the defence phase, including getting gassed in our Nuclear, Biological and Chemical warfare (NBC) suits. The rubber respirators made us look like sex gimps storming the Iranian Embassy, but the gas chamber held no fear for me. I walked into the dark room with the thick fog of CS gas as my only handrail, and was instantly reminded of my childhood living room. All that was needed was a copper spittoon full of green smoker's phlegm in the corner and it'd have brought a tear to my eye.

With our masks all fitted correctly, we had to take them off and inhale the chamber full of CS gas, which *did* bring a tear to my eye. Rioting football hooligans would probably appreciate the sting that CS gas brings. Like a swarm of bees stinging the face, the CS infuses into every facial orifice, drawing out bodily fluids that are internal for a reason.

Running out into the fresh air in a swathe of tears, snot and spit, we coughed, spluttered and gasped before breaking out into spontaneous laughter at the sight of each other: red, sweaty heads, as if apple bobbing in a deep fat fryer, blanched in a deathly pale covering of Fuller's Earth Powder and mucus.

Like having fibreglass rash, the gas required washing off with cool water. In contrast, sweating would cause the stinging itch to return with a swagger. We were so glad then that, after our cold showers, we had to run up to the top field to undertake assault engineering lessons on defensive tactics where we'd continue to sweat, bouncing out hundreds of metres of barbed dannert wire, then collecting it up to bounce it all out again, in the name of 'practice'.

The confirmatory exercise for the defensive tactics learnt was called 'Holdfast'. Yomping once more up to Woodbury Common, this time carrying a heavy weight, my shovel overhung the bottom of the poncho roll which rubbed the crease joining the top of the thigh with the bottom of my buttocks. By the time we'd covered four of the six miles, my arse had a weeping sore attaching my skin to my combats, a relationship I was rather averse to.

Navigated to a hilly area, we were positioned where trenches would have to be hand dug. Although extremely laborious and exhausting, this would present little problem if the earth were of a loam or soft-clay consistency. Typically, however, we would be defending a hill with a ratio of one part pebble to two parts rock.

Through the night we continued in pairs into the next morning, then through the afternoon. Sleep escaped us as we rushed to get the trench dug to the required standard. By the time we had covered the sleeping area and returned the topsoil, we'd been constantly digging for twenty-seven hours. If I ever had any aspirations to being an Irish navvy, then they had certainly disappeared.

My trench partner Frank was a tough-as-leather, heavily-tattooed ex-builder with biceps the size of a four-slot toaster. He was the ideal partner physically, but mentally he wasn't as robust. As I was trying to lay out my roll mat in the rubble of the sleeping trench, I noticed his shoulders shaking and a small sniffle.

'You okay, Frank?' I asked, genuinely concerned. He was crying. The trauma of the exercise had beaten him.

'Not really. It's my birthday.'

'Happy birthday,' I said gleefully, with all the tact of Enoch Powell.

He glared at me rather menacingly. 'Is it a happy birthday? I should be with my wife and kids. Not fucking here in this shithole doing this shit.' He launched the nearby pick helve skywards.

If Great Britain needed an Olympic standard hammer thrower, they could do worse than the mess that now stood before me.

'I fucking miss them. Desperately.'

Until now I'd never realised the sacrifices some of my compatriots were making. Unlike me, who had little to leave behind, some of these guys were voluntarily going through this continuous hell while sacrificing the comforts of a warm double bed, loved ones to cherish, and a real home life, all for the green beret. My respect for them soared even higher.

* * *

The week was physically draining due to sleep deprivation. It's a strange beast, bringing out odd behaviour in even the most robust of men. Charlie cackled like a witch on a night patrol for no other reason than Fred in front had a clown clinging to his back. Of course there was no clown, only webbing; but the onset of hallucinations came as a symptom of not getting any shut-eye. It was my first witnessing of hallucinatory behaviour.

Weirder still was Charlie putting out his washing in a field. There was I, settling into my sentry position as comfortably as you can on sharp rock, staring into the shallow re-entrant to my front. Even with no enemy in sight, I was particularly surprised when Charlie stood in the re-entrant with his laundry, hanging it out on a washing line.

*An odd thing to do when on exercise*, I thought, *and why on earth is he in civvies?*

'Charlie!' I called. 'What are you doing?' Even though only a few metres away, he clearly couldn't hear my call. 'Charlie!' I repeated a little louder.

'Frig me pink, Timey, you mad bastard, why are you calling Charlie?'

It was Fred from my rear.

'It's not me who's mad, it's Charlie, look, hanging out his

washing,' I said, pointing to nothing but an empty re-entrant. 'Where's he gone? I asked, rather confused.

Fred had evidently knocked me from my psychotic world back to reality, where Charlie was in a trench digging out bits of rock with laundry probably the last thing on his mind.

Hard as it was to stay awake, if we were given the alarm 'Gas! Gas! Gas!' we'd have to immediately don full NBC clothing, including our respirators, as smoke slowly drifted across our positions to simulate the creeping death of toxins such as mustard gas or sarin.

Swaddled within the warmth of full PPE with an NBC hood over a respirator cocooning the face causes a certain amount of drowsiness, even without inhaling a nerve agent. In certain casinos, piped oxygen is pushed through the air conditioning system to promote alertness, lengthening a patron's ability to spend money. Laid down on sentry, wearing a respirator on a warm spring day works in exactly the opposite way. Anyone who, after being awake for the previous twenty-seven hours, can resist succumbing to the ever-increasing weight of the head and not submit to the odd catnap is held forever in my respect.

Sticking an upright bayonet under the chin is an age-old method of preventing sleep; but if not for the fear of letting my mates down, I'd have gladly impaled my face to get a few minutes kip.

Many times we believed we were awake, stood in the trench, only to open our eyes to face a pair of boots. These would usually be attached to a member of the training team who had stood there long enough to confirm our closed eyes weren't just a long blink. Counting up our sleep indiscretions at the end of the exercise, the team thrashed us back to camp carrying all our kit.

'Time!' Corporal Hagar shouted with the expectant glee I now recognised as a precursor to pain. 'You've been caught a few times. So you can have some metal fence pickets as well.' Fence pickets were pushed down onto the top of my large pack, as he had with others caught in a state of periodic slumber. I smiled falsely so as not to advertise my despair.

'And for being caught adrift from your weapon, you can have this as well.' He dragged with him a roll of dannert barbed wire, which I can categorically confirm is, other than a burning tyre, the last thing you want to carry around your neck.

In this instance, however, my choice was limited. It was Fred who at least put a smile on my face. 'You look like a bankrupt Mr T,' he glibly noted.

With fence pickets clanking against my shoulders and barbed wire digging through the hessian sacking into my neck, the arduous yomp back was in preparation for our final period of training: the commando phase.

# ELEVEN

*'The members of the so-called Commandos behave in a particularly brutal and under-hand manner.'*
ADOLF HITLER, COMMANDO ORDER 1942

THE CONFIRMATION THAT our journey was nearly complete came via swapping our blue berets for cap comforters – the neck roll that formed into the soft triangle made famous by the *Commando* comics. Wearing the cap comforter separated those recruits who had progressed to the commando phase from those yet to reach this stage in the training. Instead of me, it would be the nods in the weeks behind who would now be stood peering over the galley balcony, watching in awe those cap comforters.

Just being in the commando phase gave us more confidence. We ran with enthusiasm, as wearing a cap comforter meant we were forbidden to walk anywhere, irrespective of the strange gaits caused by the injuries prevalent throughout the troop. However, everything previously endured in training was just the key to the hurt locker we were about to step into – it was now the dawn of true pain.

Although we had boxed and done a little wrestling, we had far more fun bending, throwing and hitting each other while learning the art of unarmed combat, hand-to-hand fighting synonymous with the commandos of old. In doing so, we discovered little-known animals: the 'wide-mouth frog' and the 'numb-armed bastard', neither of which even Sir David Attenborough would have seen. These sessions gave confidence to the least aggressive recruits, so that they could handle themselves should some Spetsnaz operator attack them with a shovel, or a smart prick in a pub launch at them with a spork.

We witnessed pig corpses blown to smithereens to give us an indication of the destruction various weapons systems could inflict upon the body. We would then patch up the wounds they had suffered. While I'm sure the training team would have like to shoot some of us, the use of a few pigs satisfied their need.

We jumped from hovering helicopters and for the first time I truly felt I was doing something special. I had never even seen a helicopter prior to joining up, other than on the telly, and just to smell their fumes gave me a twitch in my starched pants.

Back on Dartmoor we practised river crossings and cliff assaults, scaling rock faces in full kit this time, though thankfully without haemorrhoids. While very commando-like, it paled in comparison to the fun of abseiling back down. We scaled 20m up rope ladders that swung uncontrollably; while it raised the blood pressure and squeaked the sphincter, it was the most exhilaration I'd experienced since joining up.

We would ascend again in an altogether easier fashion, undertaking a roller haulage technique whereby we would be pulled vertically up the cliff by the rest of the troop at the top. It was like being at some sort of adult fairground and my face cramped with smiling so much. I couldn't believe how lucky I was, actually being paid to learn all the specialist skills required by a commando.

While all this flying around in helicopters, disarming knife-wielding attackers, abseiling down quarry walls and inspecting porcine wounds was very exciting, at the back of our minds, niggling away like a bit of steak caught between molars, we knew we'd have to soon undertake the commando tests.

These tests are the physical criteria all Royal Marines have to successfully complete in order to gain the green beret. Throughout training we had interim physical tests – basic fitness tests, USMC gym tests, battle swimming tests, IMF pass-out, BFT pass-out, four- and six-mile speed marches; but the commando tests were all important. Fail any of these and the months of training so far undertaken would have been wasted. We would get three chances at passing. If deemed unfit to succeed we'd be given a ticket home, a failed wannabe commando with only futile excuses.

\* \* \*

## The Commando Tests
## Endurance Course

Only ever run when the weather is insufferable, the course starts on Woodbury Common at 07.45, so an early-morning four-mile speed walk is required through the fog of vapourised breath to reach the start line. Even this is an important part of the test; not only does it give us time to make sure our weapon is secured comfortably and our fighting order is snug by the application of bungee cords wrapped around our webbing to mitigate friction, but it also provides a mental battle to overcome the fear of what we know lays ahead.

The first part of the endurance course is a series of tunnels and obstacles, acts of calculated sadism. Okay, so I didn't expect the tunnel designers to make them luxurious transit points adorned with animal skin rugs. But it would have been nice if the floors were designed as a muddy mess smooth enough to slide through. Instead, some sadist had the marvellous idea of shovelling shitloads of sharp shingle in there to destroy what is left of your knees.

'The shingle is there to aid drainage,' we were told by a PTI. Yet every time I went through any tunnel, I nearly drowned in the fetid, foul-smelling water. Depending on size, a recruit either manages to crawl, each movement creating painful spasms, or the bigger lads slide through like epileptic eels, webbing and weapon crashing on the tunnel's corrugated tin sides sounding like a skeleton wanking in a dustbin.

The first obstacle is called the 'dry tunnel', named by someone with a vocational qualification in irony. It was always so wet that if I looked at it for too long I feared I might develop trench eye.

Running down a dip over rough terrain causes the knees to scream before entering Peter's pool. I never found out who Peter was, but I think he was a little careless leaving a pool there in the middle of the endurance course; it just got in the way.

Although I was never fortunate enough, like some, to have the privilege of breaking the ice on its surface, we did witness thin, frozen slivers on its edges. Entering the icy-cold water, lungs implode automatically, forcing gasps of exhaling air. Inhaling is made all the more difficult when the throat is blocked by rocketing testicles.

To those vertically challenged such as I, the pool is neck deep. Lurching along the sunken rope is easy; exiting isn't. Bodyweight doubles from the inundating water, just the tonic running up a forty-five degree hill of shale and mud that, although short, immediately steals away any bounding energy.

Just as heavy breathing reaches a modicum of normalcy, along comes the water tunnel. It is a submerged pipe that a recruit must individually torpedo through. Here, underwater in darkness, the senses are reduced and those submerged are totally reliant on colleagues at each end of the tunnel engaged in a push me/pull me drill. The human torpedo hopes not to get jagged on some randomly placed obstruction, as the tunnel's girth is too narrow to allow any freeing movement should they get stuck. If Peter's pool doesn't saturate, then the water tunnel does.

Being submerged in dirty brown water leaves not an inch of

the body dry. The squelching of wet boots sliding irregularly over slimy mud and ankle-turning rocks is the syncopated backing track to the drumbeat of drenched webbing bouncing off blistered backs; rasping breath adds the vocals.

The next area that could cause anyone to come a cropper is the sheep dip, a gully of ankle-deep water and energy-sapping deep mud, with banks that, if not approached correctly, lead to a comedy slip. Not funny if it happens to you, just more energy wasted when at an absolute premium.

Through the woods of Woodbury Common, the next obstacle is the claustrophobe's nemesis – a 30m water pipe, known as the 'smartie tube'. It envelops the biggest blokes, who struggle to fit their wide shoulders and kit through. In winter, when the water is high, and when we do it, it always is; (I can only imagine the training team filling it with a hose in the summer) the excess water means I literally have I had to drag myself unceremoniously through the near-darkness, scraping my nose along the roof to obtain air along with mouthfuls of mudded slurry. Fresh air is welcome upon exiting, unlike the pain from the crawling.

We carry on again; even trying to stand upright after the smartie tube is an effort, but we ignore our self-mutilation. We thankfully reach the final obstacle, the zigzag tunnel, sponsored by knee-reconstruction surgeons. While we can't shoot through it, the zigzag tunnel is probably the least distressing obstacle.

Upon exiting, a member of the training team will check an individual's weapon for blockages and offer some sarcastic remark, before a limp up a slow, grinding, dirt-track hill sees knackered yet determined bodies reach the metal road where begins the four-mile run back to camp in full, wet, heavy and uncomfortable kit.

It is here, where forestry turns into farmland, that the recruits split up. Throughout the obstacle phase, teamwork is encouraged by sticking together to assist each other through the difficulties. Now it is every man for himself to attain the best time possible.

The key is to quickly develop a rhythm, to synchronise bounding legs, pumping arms and lung-filling breaths that inhale the pungent perfumery of steaming cow shit and farm slurry that attracts a haze of flying insects intent on dive bombing eyeballs or open mouths. Often my rhythm is similar to a tachycardia-suffering tortoise and even the downhill stretches caused me to dribble mud and the odd fly I'd so far consumed.

On Heartbreak Lane – a rather literal name for a road so cruel – 500m before we reach CTC a sign hangs from a tree. Painted on it is a comedy-caricature marine gasping and puffing with the immortal words, 'It's Only Pain.' It is a shout of encouragement to strengthen the resolve of those who pass it. For me, it always works.

The overpass footbridge outside CTC becomes an impromptu obstacle; it has just the right amount of steps to kill any energy left in the thighs, dribble phlegm over the railings onto passing cars underneath, then to painfully jar the already destroyed knee cartilage on the downward steps.

The finish line of the endurance course is at the far end of CTC, where success is dependent on getting six out of ten shots on target at the 25m weapon range. As the easiest part of the course, if the weapon jams due to any serious damage sustained through the rigours of the tunnels, it results in a sickening fail. All the previous suffering, all the heartache leading up to this point, would be in vain.

Pass times have changed over the decades due to changes of route, but completing the course in less than seventy-one minutes was our target.

## Tarzan Assault Course

Imagine being Spider-Man, flying high through the air, jumping sprightly to swing, balance and launch yourself from one structure to another. Now imagine doing that wearing boots better designed for diving, with a weapon continually clattering against the back of your head and 16kg of weight bouncing off your midriff. Spider-Man never did, the wanker. And he wore spandex.

The Tarzan assault is a high obstacle course of ropes, swings and nets that challenges both physical co-ordination and mental courage. Starting on the aptly-named Death Slide, recruits whizz from the 15m high tower down the manila rope, then take on the various high-wire, rope, beam and ladder disciplines interwoven between the ancient trees that make up a giant sized version of the board game 'Mouse Trap. Falling from any discipline would not necessarily fail anyone; however, if anyone could walk away from a fall and still eat solids, he is a better man than me.

When completing the Tarzan phase, a 150m run leads to

the assault course that a recruit has run around many times before. Having the Tarzan as a warm-up tends to make the assault course a tad more difficult, but as is often the case, mental strength is the spur to continue onwards to the final obstacle – the 30ft wall that is climbed using a rope for assistance. On reaching the top, the recruit gives their name with the most triumphant shout they can muster.

One of my fellow recruit's surnames was Thorpe. It is a verbal blur, a rather bland, soft monosyllable that is difficult to understand through a thick Welsh accent and heavy breaths.

'Thorpe, Corporal!' he would gasp.

'Fox?'

'No, Thorpe, Corporal!'

'Fawn?'

It continued through 'Thorn? Thought? Halt? Fawlty?' until Thorpe realised the PTI was just taking the piss. His finish times were always thirty seconds longer than they should have been after the PTI's verbal jousting.

Thirteen minutes of speed, strength, agility, and correctly pronouncing your surname will lead to passing the Tarzan assault course.

## The Nine-Mile Speed March

The least spectacular of the tests, the 'nine-miler' is a straight speed march over splendid hills and through wondrous dells of the Devon countryside. By now speed marching has become as natural as waking up in agony, but as a pass-out test it is done at a more breakneck speed than necessary. Ninety minutes at a ten-minute-mile speed would see a recruit troop home, but most do it far quicker.

The nine-mile finish only becomes the start line for a long troop attack where a fictitious enemy seems to be an infinite distance away – coincidentally up a hill, never at the far end of a bowling green. Even without a false-dawn finish a recruit will continue in formation, dashing down, crawling, taking cover, observing sight, time and time again, the recruit wishing every dive will be the last. In the real world, it is pointless speed marching to an objective and being unable to carry out the necessary assault once there.

As a recruit, there is no better way to finish a Saturday morning than the 'nine-miler.' All there is left to complete the tests and earn the green beret is the final small task: the 'thirty-miler'.

## The Thirty-Mile March

With an evening of route planning complete, personal administration consists of ensuring kit is well fitting, eating as much as possible and taping up the majority of bare flesh to reduce contact sores. With the variety of burns, blisters and bruises on my battered body, by the time I finished I looked more like an Egyptian mummy than a nod.

Waking in the dark, a hearty breakfast is all that is required before greeting the harsh bleakness of Dartmoor, which at first light has an unnerving tranquillity. In syndicates of eight, all assist in the navigation of the march accompanied by a corporal who, rather than giving permanent bollockings, now carries a couple of jars of encouragement.

The march takes in some of the most breathtakingly beautiful parts of the moor, as well as the wettest. Already raw feet soon become wet crossing streams early in the route. Marching speedily from checkpoint to checkpoint, never settling for more than a couple of minutes to prevent bodies stiffening, recruits take in sweet, stewed tea and sandwiches, whilst cajoling and encouraging each other.

At mile twenty-six, the recruits steam over the highest point on southern Dartmoor, Ryder's Hill. Due to its convex shape, no matter how many times the recruits think they have reached the top, there is yet another summit to conquer; however, with the finish in my day at Cross Furzes, just over the other side of the hill, they would willingly drag their bollocks over broken glass to get there.

Marching over the soft moor takes its toll on thighs, the hard metal roads take their revenge on feet, but the last few steps to the finish are taken on a cushion of euphoria. Crossing the thirty miles of rough Dartmoor terrain in less than eight hours would see a recruit pass the final commando test.

\* \* \*

Taken individually, each test is eminently achievable. Anyone with a high standard of fitness, no injuries and a good period of balanced preparation could successfully complete each challenge. The difference for us as Royal Marine recruits is that we were twenty-five weeks into a highly demanding training course. Although our fitness has been equated with that of an Olympic athlete, our bodies were stock cars, getting battered from one heavy crash to another. With little time for rest and recuperation, injuries were common and recurrent. The options were limited – push through the pain barrier, or be back trooped. The latter would only mean prolonging the torture.

The commando phase meant we wouldn't do each test just the once. We would practise them repeatedly, thus degrading our bodies even further.

Test week, where each test would follow on consecutive days, would commence the day after we returned from the final exercise – a twelve-day consolidation of everything we had learned in military training.

Our fitness was now only part of what was necessary to complete the commando phase. Mental fortitude and the will to push beyond our pain and fatigue thresholds were equally, if not more, important.

\* \* \*

The final exercise was now upon us. We saw it closing in as we counted down the days. It stared at us from the schedule pinned to the wall in pink paper, which I can only assume was to soften the blow. I hated looking at it. I hoped if I closed my eyes it would go away and become something far more pleasurable when I opened them. But there it still was. They could have named it something like Exercise Final Hurdle or Exercise Well Done Lads You're Nearly There, but no. They called it Exercise Nightmare – and with good reason.

It started out as a bit of a dream. We were taken in a plush coach down to Portsmouth to spend a day out learning about naval and Royal Marines history. We walked around HMS Victory and the Royal Marines Museum at Eastney Barracks feeling like tourists, although I was a little despondent I couldn't buy an ice cream.

We moved to RM Poole to meet blokes from our very own Special Forces, the SBS. We looked in awe at these guys who, in our commando-tastic fantasies, all had webbed feet, gills and black masking tape covering their eyes.

Disappointingly, they looked like normal blokes, although it has to be said it seemed their selection into SB was dependent on them being suave dreamboats. I made a note to check up on cosmetic surgery services should I ever want to go SF.

We moved on to watch a demo by the less revered driver's branch, who took us on combat log flumes when driving through deep water in Land Rovers. We were mightily impressed and choked by one marine burning rubber as he screeched around the skid pan circuit completing J and S turns, evasive driving techniques we'd only seen on *Starsky and Hutch*. It was all extremely impressive and rather distinct from the drivers we had so far met at CTC, who looked as bored as bat shit dropping off nods on Woodbury Common.

The one part of commando operations we had yet to be exposed to was the amphibious capability the Corps uniquely holds. We zoomed about on rigid raiders and sat bobbing in landing craft, jumping into the icy waters of Hamworthy harbour to make beach landings. Like the day spent climbing cliffs, all this rugsy-tugsy, commando-type stuff I had seen in the recruitment brochures was even more brilliant in real life.

But all this frivolity had to come to an end.

The troop sergeant called us together for a snap parade instead of the planned visit to the NAAFI. We stood nervously as he paced up and down like a father outside a labour ward, only with anger not nerves. I don't think I was the only one expecting to hear the words 'stand by'.

'You fucking lot are in the deepest fucking shit I think I have ever fucking seen. I assure you, you are going to be thrashed until your eyes bleed.'

It wasn't the most pleasant of openings. We sort of guessed why we had been called together.

Many of us had gone to Exeter to buy lots of green string. As an extra special treat, we purchased civilian boots to wear on the exercise. We knew that as soon as we went to commando units we would buy our own.

In fact, very little clothing worn in a commando unit, when in the field, is military issue. We just thought we were exceedingly switched on in pre-empting this by purchasing boots while still recruits. Having only taken our new civilian boots to Poole, the training team couldn't make us wear our issue pair. Not having control over this made them very angry. Very angry indeed.

The troop sergeant's head had turned the colour of an overripe aubergine. We had often seen him angry, it was far more common than him being happy, but the spittle from his crooked mouth told us this was a new level of fury.

'You think you are fucking clever buying these fucking Carlos Fandango boots. When your feet are being cut to fucking shreds by wearing these new fucking Gucci boots, don't even fucking think about coming to fucking whinge. I cannot describe my loathing for you fuckers. You literally are a bunch of cunts. You fucking fuckers can fucking stand by to stand by. If I had my fucking way the lot of you would be fucking back trooped. Now fuck off and prepare for severe unpleasantness.'

There was a swear jar somewhere that was willing to be filled.

His threats were not idle. Instead of starting the exercise with a morning twelve-mile insertion yomp, we set out the night before and were taken by landing craft to an unknown point. It was like one of those mystery tours at the seaside, only we were fairly sure it wouldn't end with a nice meal at a pub.

When we reached our destination, the coxswain pointed in the direction we needed to head as the ramp lowered. The wind swirled inside and the temperature plummeted. Sea spray welcomed us to the gates of a freezing Hades.

'Out troops,' he shouted.

As good recruits do, we obeyed the order to disembark – into rather deep water. It was far deeper than I expected. In fact I was up to my neck in cold seawater, full kit and all. I had to bounce to ensure I didn't go under and the pull of the current sent me slightly off track. It was rather unnerving until I finally managed to breathlessly struggle ashore.

We rendezvoused in a slightly submerged area covered by reeds. The training team then informed us we would be picked up tomorrow. They were leaving us to freeze our tits off.

'Your new boots should keep you warm,' was the last dose of sarcasm we received as they disappeared towards the teasing urban warmth.

We had dry kit in our waterproofed bergans. But was it wise to change into them? We were in cold seawater surrounded by the warmth of sodden, marshy reeds, the cold wind as welcome as a matador at a vegan conference. Putting on dry kit would only mean drenching both sets of clothing, going against all the rules of the wet/dry routine we had been taught.

We had to tough it out in wet gear, so we lay shivering in the reeds all night. It was a long, cold, sleepless night, and despondency kicked me up the arse yet again when I realised the gloves in my pocket were drenched – a prophetic start to Exercise Nightmare.

The training team arrived at first light. I had never been so happy to see those bastards. We dragged ourselves back out to the landing craft and were taken to our original point to embark on our aptly-named exercise.

The twelve-mile insertion yomp was counted as the first actual commando test, even if it was just a warm-up to the final exercise. Normally yomping such a distance wouldn't have been an issue, but we'd now forsaken large packs and were issued proper 120-litre bergans. Three times as much space to put three times as much kit in to make it three times as heavy and, as I'd experienced the previous night, three times as difficult to drag through reeds. But it felt far more comfortable than the crippling packs we had used up to now, even if we were saturated.

Crotch rot soon followed, with saggy, wet combats rubbing my inner thighs, each step shaving off just a little more skin – just what I needed on the first day of an exercise. I can't remember hoping for unseasonably cold weather either, but I got it all the same. Laying up in preparation for a night raid on HMS Osprey, I contemplated whether I'd come close to hypothermia.

Charlie woke me for the assault but I couldn't find my balance, inertia stupefying me. He held me up and asked if I was okay. Of course I said yes, but I couldn't feel my feet and hands and had a strange unease I'd never encountered before.

Frost had settled on the ground and my throat rasped when I inhaled. Just to move seemed an effort and as I rolled up my mat, leaving a dark patch on the frosted ground, I tried unsuccessfully to shelter myself from the icy winds that blew from the English Channel onto the exposed heights of Portland Bill.

Even now, I look back and consider this to be the point where I experienced the very coldest conditions. Yet pushing through this discomfort and pain is what makes a commando, someone who can take the extreme hardship and carry on. When the seeds of doubt are sown in the mind, it takes willpower and courage to press on regardless.

With the thoughts of coldness stowed away with the rest of my kit, I loved attacking the base – especially as we made a matelot shit himself when storming his sentry post full of chocolate wrappers and pornography. We moved further southwest by helicopter. For the duration of the exercise we would endure extreme Dartmoor weather.

'It's as cold as a bastard,' commented Fred, as we looked through squinted eyes over the whitened bleakness. I couldn't have put it better myself.

Heavy blizzards forced us to plough unceremoniously through knee high snow, trying to make good speed wherever we advanced to contact. The awaiting enemy, played by the specialist unit of marines, must have been freezing their tits off by the time we arrived. One actually went down with hypothermia.

The weather was relentless, pelting us with freezing hail one minute then shrouding us in snow the next. The cowardly sun didn't have the balls to shine through the greyness. Our jokes were diminishing and the only smiles were grins of perseverance to get through this communal hell.

I had been sharing a bivvy with Fred, as I often did. At first we were like two naughty schoolboys who would giggle at the slightest oddity, should it be someone falling over or quite pitiful jokes taken straight from The Shit Joke Annual 1987.

As the days wore us down I could see Fred's cheerfulness ebbing away, something noted by the training team, who themselves must have wondered who they'd upset to be present on the moor in such conditions. They pulled Fred away for a while and he returned as he had left, a shivering wreck. His behaviour had become a concern to the team and they were worried he had succumbed to the conditions, but Fred had convinced them he was fine to continue. After all, one of the symptoms of hypothermia is mental confusion, something that Fred could present even on a warm summer's day.

However, his inability to rise from his sleeping bag for a later sentry meant I had to cover for him, something the beady eyes of the training team did not miss. In a role reversal of Captain Oates' fateful last walk, I told Fred, as I trudged away towards the sentry position, that I wouldn't be long. On my return an hour later, the bivvy was empty. He was gone.

The training team saw his withdrawal as a final confirmation of hypothermia, the green light to take him from the moor and back to a warm bed in sickbay. It was exceedingly hard on Fred, and if I were to be honest, on me as well; my morale boost had gone. Missing even a few hours to reheat the body would see him fail the exercise.

A few of the other recruits also succumbed to the cold, taken back to the comfortable bosom of civilisation. Nods were dropping like flies from the harshest of climates. Even sadder still, a few hours later, despite my best efforts in trying to cheer him with my crap jokes about dogs and pants, Charlie had also been taken off the moor. I watched him leave, his shivering body working in slow motion, dizziness causing him to stumble like a drunk. My two best mates had been taken from me.

The bastion of mateship had already been breached, but I paired up with a new bivvy partner. As a Scotsman and Englishman together, we embraced our resilience, recognising that if we too were to succumb to the cold we'd only have to do it all again. Mind you, for him, being from Inverness, it must have been like a summer's day.

The cold dissipated on the final evening, to be replaced by torrential rain. Dry cold then rain is dangerous enough, but if the cold snap returned after such a downpour then many more of us would be in danger of hypothermia. I think even the training team were looking forward to the exercise ending. We had it hard, but they too had also to endure the weather. While they were seasoned veterans, slowly picking off hypothermic nods from the moor was not good for their morale.

It must have been due to this rush to get things over and done with when Corporal Hagar hurriedly pushed me from a wall we were traversing. With a GPMG in my arms and a fully loaded bergan on my back, I fell awkwardly. Immediately, I knew my ankle wasn't in a good state.

I could have cursed him, called him names that my gran would have given me a thick ear over and, under my breath, I probably did. But, trashed ankle or not, I was determined to finish. No way was I going to repeat this exercise.

With an increasingly sore ankle, I finished the exercise at Bickleigh Barracks, marching into 42 Commando's home, watching the marines laugh at us as we walked in as proficiently as we could. The morning had started with a dawn attack on an old fort, then ended in a speed march to finish there, where tepid sausage, beans and egg had never tasted so good and the hot showers felt like ambrosia poured by the gods themselves onto our tired and grimy bodies.

Part one – to my mind, the hardest test of the commando phase – was thankfully over. Returning to CTC a conquering hero, my first port of call was to see if Charlie and Fred were okay. Unfortunately, they had already left to do the exercise all over again. I couldn't think of a worse way to spend the next fortnight, other than to boil my head in a cauldron of piss.

As for me, even without the benefit of a medical practitioner's qualification, I knew something was definitely not right. As I made my ravenous way from Fred and Charlie's accommodation it became increasingly difficult to bear weight on my foot and by the time I had reached the galley doors I was hopping, the pain unbearable. Like most, I hit my bed early, hoping I was just suffering post-exercise soreness.

The next morning I woke up and felt little pain in my ankle. But on trying to get out of bed I feared the worst. The pain became hideous when trying to bear my weight, and the ankle had swollen to the size of a black and bruised melon (a honeydew, not a watermelon – that would be an exaggeration). I showed the training team who, to be fair, suggested I report sick, leaving me safe in the knowledge I wouldn't be doing the Tarzan assault pass-out later in the day. I had pretty much deduced that, anyway.

I limped pathetically for what seemed like miles to the sickbay and was treated by a medic, who immediately called the doc.

'Hmmm,' he said, tapping a pencil against his cheek.

'*Aaagh*,' I screamed, as he prodded my ankle.

'Does that hurt?' he asked stupidly.

'Uh yes, Sir.' Being facetious without sounding insubordinate was a riddle in terms of intonation, but I think I got away with it.

'Hmmm,' he annoyingly repeated, studying my half-naked body.

'*Aaagh*,' I screamed again as he pressed my pelvis. He didn't ask me again if I had felt any pain.

'Well, the good news is you haven't broken your ankle.'

That was a relief; it would have been three months in rehabilitation, possibly shoving me into the ranks of 'perma-nod' – the name given to recruits spending more than a year at CTC.

'Have you heard of Woodbury rot?' The Doc was up to his old tricks again.

'Yes, Sir.'

'Well, by the look of things, that's what you've got.'

'But I was on Dartmoor, Sir.' It was my turn to take up the idiot baton.

'It isn't exclusive to one training area, but could have been incubated from the endurance course or somewhere else. Either way you've got it. See this painful lump here in your pelvis?' He prodded it again just to ensure I hadn't forgotten it was painful. 'It's a lymph gland fighting the infection. You've got an ankle full of poison. Lucky you haven't succumbed to septicaemia. You can die from that.'

A double relief then – no broken ankle and I was alive. What a result – but the celebratory somersaults would have to wait. There was nothing else I could do but take copious amounts of drugs and lay in sickbay until it had subsided.

My world once again fell around me. Totally gutted at the news, I settled into life as a sick bay ranger in a bed with a telly. It should have been a cosy few days feeling permanently warm, having food brought to me – not by a Barbara Windsor *Carry On*-style nurse in a tight-fitting uniform, I might add, but by a burly male navy nurse looking more like Bernard Bresslaw. Yet all I wanted to do was get out of there and finish the commando tests so that this purgatory could finally end.

Other medics visited and did little to reduce my fears of a lengthy injury by taking photos of my ankle, which was acclaimed 'a beauty'. I welcomed the odd visit from fellow recruits, informing me of the gossip and how the commando tests were progressing. The compassionate training team informed me I could do my commando tests with the lads who had failed their first attempt, but would have only two attempts before getting back trooped again. Bargain.

I was discharged from sickbay on the Sunday morning of week twenty-eight. If I was to pass out with my troop I'd have to pass the commando tests prior to going on the upcoming Easter leave.

If I'd been a professional athlete there was no way I'd be even contemplating walking without the aid of crutches. Even if was a normal civilian, I'd have been given a taxi on release from hospital and told to rest for a fortnight.

Unfortunately I wasn't. I was a Royal Marines recruit on my way to do a thirty-mile march.

# TWELVE

'Son, one day you will make a girl very happy for a short period of time, then she'll leave you and be with men who are ten times better than you could ever hope to be. These men are called Royal Marines.'

ANON

THE THIRTY-MILER is the final hurdle and the test that transforms a recruit into a commando, should everything go to plan. My own plans had gone slightly awry, thanks to my immune system deciding to have a week off. So I had to attempt what is normally the final commando test first.

I staggered from my bed, like an old man with rickets, to join the troop for the route briefing for the following morning's thirty-miler. I was popping strong antibiotic pills and painkillers, so I thought a quick phone call to Exeter air traffic control would be in order as I'd be flying over Dartmoor.

And I virtually did. I wasn't the only one on medication, a few lads had shin splints, another had inflamed Achilles' tendonitis. To be honest, we were all being a bit soft – some guys had completed the thirty-miler with broken limbs.

The weather was typical Dartmoor, having five seasons in one day, including the lesser-known 'honking' season. Ignoring whatever weather was thrown at me, I felt good, as one does when doped up to the eyeballs, and confident we could comfortably complete within the time.

'How's the ankle coping, Time?' asked the troop PTI.

'Fine, Corporal.'

'Any pain?'

'Not now, Corporal. The pain from my blisters bursting has taken over.'

'That's the spirit. Crack on.'

Full of spirit, we conquered Ryder's Hill and, forgetting the pain in our knees as we descended to Cross Furzes, saw the end in sight. Finishing in just over seven hours, we ran towards the small gathering that greeted us.

The final metres of the thirty-miler is always lined with green-bereted commandos applauding those finishing. It is a salute to completion of the longest infantry training in NATO, and a welcome for those who will now stand by their side – an elite band of brothers that has few peers.

Halting as if we were on the drill square, rather than completing a lengthy march over Dartmoor, we were split into two groups. I was part of the group still to pass all the tests and so was put on the flank of shame. Green berets were handed out to those who had successfully completed the previous tests. I was genuinely happy for them, but felt wholly envious and left out as the berets were placed upon the heads of those who'd earned them. Finishing the thirty-miler should be the pinnacle of training. For me it was a hollow victory.

Returning to CTC in the back of the four-tonne truck, the mood was high. Everyone had passed the thirty-miler and, in truth, we'd all found it far easier than expected. Those who had passed all the tests were especially buoyant. They knew that, barring a cataclysmic event, in two weeks they would be passing out as Royal Marine Commandos.

In the morning we would be officially in King's Squad, dressed permanently in drill uniform. Their final two weeks would be spent on the drill square, practising for their pass-out parade. I, however, would be getting back into my beasting jacket and taking on the Tarzan assault course with the failures from the previous week's test.

There were only the three of us lined up at the foot of the death slide. I already knew I wouldn't pass. My ankle had survived the thirty-miler by drugs and courage, but the rest afterwards had returned me to a pain level similar to that suffered after the final exercise.

Mental discipline, fortitude and mind over matter are easier said than done when you can hardly walk. Telling the accompanying troop officer that I wasn't fit to do it never even crossed my mind, but as I jumped into the first net the pain was too much. I staggered along the high wires feeling nauseous, but set off towards the assault course.

'Time, stop. You're finished,' the troop officer shouted from behind.

I was nowhere near finished.

'Time,' the shout came louder this time. 'I said you're finished. Stop.'

I struggled on regardless at the speed of an arthritic octogenarian. Tears welled up in my eyes, and my teeth were gritted so hard my jaw ached. The shouts got louder and angrier. I stopped. I was so close to getting that green beret I could taste it, yet all that lay on my tongue was the salt of tears. I had broken down again, physically and now mentally. I had regressed to a young boy with failure as his constant sidekick, weeping inconsolably.

'Listen,' ordered the troop officer with a hint of sympathy.

My head refused to draw away from the floor, the only place I could bear to look.

'Look at me, Time.'

I raised my head. He put his arm on my shoulder.

'Look, Time, you're already near the time limit. There's no way you can make it. I can't see you carrying on and suffering like this. All you're going to do is totally fuck yourself up. You will have to get yourself sorted and then have another crack with another troop. You're in no fit state to pass now.'

Like an old horse, my time was up. He was sending me to the knacker's yard. I was being back trooped – again.

My mind swirled, not accepting the day's events. I cleared out my belongings to retreat to a spare room of my new troop, still away on Exercise Nightmare. I was back trooped with a fellow injured recruit called Lee. While it was tough on us both, having someone else who was going through the same agony made it easier to bear. As I could see the finish line, with Easter leave approaching, I found myself trying not to be too despondent.

\* \* \*

Joining my new colleagues of 523 Troop was a far easier experience than I'd imagined. Many were lads from the troop I had just left. They had either been back trooped earlier in training or been taken off my final exercise, so I knew many already – including Fred and Charlie.

Out of the fifty-two that had started with 523 Troop, only four originals remained. This was not only testament to these lads' incredible durability, but the demands placed upon all those who pass through CTC. Having such small numbers remaining was not unusual. Some troops even had to be amalgamated if natural selection devastated two consecutive troops' numbers to insufficient levels.

For the hierarchy it was, and always will be, a fine balancing act between maintaining a training regime harsh enough to separate the wheat from the chaff and the demands of the Treasury, who want value for money in their forces. Having fifty-two commence training, for only four to finish, could seem to a Saville Row suited bean counter sat comfortably at his leather trimmed desk in his plush Whitehall office a terrible waste of taxpayers' money.

With Easter upon us, the troop I'd just left invited me to their King's Squad piss-up – a night out where the lads could see a more humane side to the training team and we could get absolutely rat-arsed with no civvies to offer complaint.

For some odd reason, we decided to have our piss-up in Okehampton Battle Camp. The only reason I can imagine we'd do this would be to see the two women regarded as the world's ugliest strippers. As my sexual experience up to now had been a bit rubbish, the sight of a naked, cellulite-ridden, middle-aged woman rubbing her crusty vagina near my face, wafting her scent and overused cheap perfume, was nearly enough to put me off women for life.

\* \* \*

Returning home on leave, I was quite happy to tell friends of my injury. After all, it would only confirm how hard Royal Marines training really was. I would have liked to tell my mum something similar, but that proved problematic – I didn't have a fucking clue where she was.

I'd taken the chartered train like all the other nods to get us 'up the line', alighting at Leeds Central station as per normal. My mum and stepdad's fish and chip shop had evidently just opened. The shop-front window was filled by a queue of those who had eaten chips for lunch and now hankered after something more substantial – maybe fish and chips. Not wanting to disturb their metronomic fish-frying system, I diverted my route via the rear garden and dog shit minefield, entering through the backdoor. I immediately smelled a rat and it wasn't the battered variety new to the menu.

All houses have a smell distinctive to the occupying family, an olfactory homing beacon of familiarity. I wasn't responding to this one.

As a child living with my grandparents, the kitchen smell in my early years would usually be of skinned rabbits. Once my grandfather had died, it was just my gran and I living there. The kitchen was no longer a slaughterhouse for bunnies, and so became a makeshift toilet. As she got older Gran struggled to walk two flights of stairs to the loo, so she decided to pee in a bucket. This bucket also became a makeshift ashtray for the Senior Service habit that left her with a shock of yellow nicotine in her grey hair.

Having such a large urine collecting receptacle wouldn't have been a problem - cooking and washing with a nicotine diffused piss bucket nearby was, I am sure, common in many kitchens. Probably not so many had a young lad, running around thinking he was Kevin Keegan, kicking a small football around. My skills were pretty good but on occasion, I would batter the ball and knock over the bucket. Once knocked over, a sea of brown piss and fag ends would wash all over the kitchen floor.

If it was possible to make a floor covering that was perfect for catching, and holding urine, yet virtually impossible to clean, then the beaded linoleum mat that was stuck to the floor tiles in our kitchen would be it. Often my gran would squelch along the mat, tramping soggy fag butts underfoot to feed me my usual evening meal of coffee and bourbon biscuits.

Now, when passing a tramp in a doorway my olfactory homing beacon kicks in. And people today panic about not sterilising their kitchen tops.

So here, as I stood at the backdoor of the fish and chip shop, my senses were out of synch. The odour wasn't familiar. Even with a topping of grease, fresh cod and batter, there was something different. The strange woman who came into the back hallway was as shocked as I. A Mexican stand-off between two puzzled strangers ensued.

'What are you doing?' she asked quite politely, considering the circumstances.

'What am I doing? What are *you* doing here more like?' I replied, not quite as politely.

Once I'd prevented her husband from attacking me with a fish-filleting knife, it transpired that my mum and stepdad had not long moved house. They had upped sticks and gone, without so much as a carrier-pigeon message to tell me.

The rather bemused couple allowed me to use their phone to ring an aunt who informed me my loving family had bought a café in Scarborough, but she didn't know which one. It couldn't be that hard, surely, to find a café in the largest seaside resort town in Northeast England?

It was now 6.30pm (or 18.30 as I'd now say if someone asked, 'Time check?'). I could either get on a train to Scarborough to try to find my errant parents, or I could stay the night in Leeds. Too tight to find an overpriced hotel, I thought sleeping rough an acceptable alternative. Having just spent ten days sleeping in the frost of Dartmoor, a night on a park bench with my bergan for an oversized pillow was luxury itself.

A late spring morning in Scarborough is awash with sunburnt people promenading in silly hats, children sucking on teeth-melting confectionary for their breakfast and old people sunbathing in their cardigans talking about immigrants and the ungodly cost of a tin of beans. There is little more English than the smell of candyfloss, burgers and the North

Sea, even at 10am (or 10 hundred hours as I'd say when again asked to 'Time check?' I would also tell them it was about time they bought a watch.)

This seaside ambience would have been perfect if it wasn't raining, if I didn't have a fucked ankle and wasn't limping around trying to find people who were apparently still legally responsible for me.

To add insult to literal injury, I was humping a full bergan on my back and, in a moment of financial madness, had bought a diving suit complete with full weight belt. I was now carrying that as well, which encouraged me to sweat just a little.

Although I'd been to Scarborough a few times I'd never previously noticed how hilly it was. Then again, I had never had to walk around with a house on my back. Looking around, it did dawn on me that with the plethora of bed and breakfast joints I really should have chosen this option over a freezing night in a drug-riddled park.

Peering into every open café, I tramped frustratedly up Castle Road, a main thoroughfare in the town. As I trudged further up the hill towards the castle, there they stood behind the counter, laughing and joking with customers obviously partial to my mum's French fancies and my stepdad's tales of smashing up Paris in 1975 as a Leeds United football hooligan.

Mum greeted me warmly, totally oblivious to my travails. 'Ooh, hello love,' she said without a care in the world, bless her.

'So here you are. Is there any reason why you didn't inform me you were moving?' Under the circumstances I thought it a pretty understandable question.

'Well, we were going to.'

'Well you were going to... but...?'

*Your pen ran out? Aliens abducted you? You suddenly had a temporary bout of myotonic dystrophy?*

I should have just said, 'You are the world's shittest parents.'

A more pathetic excuse I couldn't have imagined. It would have resulted in a severe beasting if they'd been nods in the Corps. Unfortunately they weren't, so I huffily retreated to my room full of unpacked boxes on a bed that was supposedly for me, dreaming of my mother doing star jumps and my stepdad running up a hill on Dartmoor with a café chair above his head.

Despite only being there a short while, they had already built up a small band of regulars who'd come in each morning to have their arteries thickened by mum's full English breakfast. One such customer was a guy called Kim. A rather large chap, he claimed to have been in the Paras with impressive military credentials.

Kim took me under his wing when we met. I was a young, impressionable Royal Marines recruit, so wet behind the ears I had fungus, and therefore believed everything Kim would tell me. I was his mate, he kept repeating – in hindsight a little too often.

He worked on the doors of a 'fun pub' in Scarborough, so I stuck with him. He would let me in without needing any ID, as I was his mate. I listened to his tales of derring-do, Falklands War heroics, and how he was generally the hardest man in NATO.

His dad apparently owned a large army surplus store in hometown Newcastle, so he could get me lots of 'Gucci' military kit really cheap, as I was his mate. I had no hesitation in handing him £100 – a fortnight's wages to me – so he could make me look like RoboMarine when I passed out and got drafted to a commando unit.

He even invited me to a big party he had organised where loads of hot, military-loving chicks were going to be, as I was his mate. Great! A proper party with grownups!

The party consisted of Kim, me, two girls from the fun pub and a cassette of Michael Jackson's *Bad* album. I felt as uncomfortable as the two girls who were reluctant to dance with Kim, a very poor substitute for Jacko. He was more Peter Sutcliffe.

The girls left quite quickly, and I began to wonder what sort of bloke Kim really was. A few days later I called in to see him. I'd tried to distance myself but had left my expensive watch there after the crap party.

There was no answer at his apartment. I knocked on the next door; it belonged to a girl I'd met on occasion, so I expected a smiling welcome.

'You fucking bastard!' she screamed, at a volume you know others can hear. 'If you don't tell me where he is I swear I'll call the coppers and get you done as well.'

My conflict management skills not yet polished, I struggled to fathom her ire. Not the most eloquent of communicators, all I could come back with was, 'What the fuck are you on about?'

'Don't protect him. You're his brother. You know where he is, the fucking thieving bastard.'

'Firstly, I'm not his brother. Secondly…'

I didn't have a 'secondly'. My mouth was well and truly in

front of my brain and didn't really comprehend the situation. I calmed slightly.

'I've just come to get my watch from him. I left it here the other day.'

As I was believable, her anger subsided. Kim and I did have different accents and, unless I was the crappiest burglar ever, I'd hardly return to the scene of the crime within a few days.

'So what's happened?'

'We must have all been at work when he came, 'cos when we all returned our flats had been broken into, including mine. He's robbed everyone, turned over all our private stuff, went through me knicker drawer and he even broke open the gas and leccy meters.'

'Frigging hell, that's awful. But how do you know it was him?'

'When the coppers came, they checked his flat. He'd cleared out all of his stuff and done a runner, so it was obviously him. That's not the worst of it, though. The only thing left was his bed. Guess what they found underneath it?'

'A watch and some military clothing?' I asked hopefully.

'No, a claw hammer and a crow bar.'

'Ah, the toolkit of any self-respecting serial killer,' I replied, an attempt at levity.

'It's not fucking funny, he's nicked all me vibrators.'

Now that was funny.

In the vain hope he may have left some stuff other than sex toys, I tracked down the two girls from the fun pub. Unsurprisingly, he'd left nothing for me but left them with tall tales of going on a secret mission in Angola.

If Kim was ever in the military, it seemed he was the sort that the establishment probably wish they had never trained. He was a walking argument for the introduction of psychological profiling.

Years later, a programme was screened documenting a group of ragtag mercenaries fighting in the Balkans, doing their utmost to become a laughing stock to anyone with even a week's worth of military training. My jaw literally dropped when the main character turned out to be a big, fat Geordie called Kim. He even got a book deal out of it, so I hope a hundred quid from the royalties he earned is winging its way in the post to me. I've been waiting a while, so I'll blame the Royal Mail.

Despite getting matey with a maniac, being laid up at home was becoming a bore. So I did what any seventeen-year-old Royal Marines recruit would do to aid the recovery of his sore ankle: I ran eighteen miles with a bergan on my back.

Initially, I only planned to run to Filey, some eight miles away. Yet as I passed the lines of caravan parks with impressionable teenage girls looking from afar, thinking I was some sort of super-marine or sweat-drenched imbecile, I felt good. So good, in fact, I carried on to the small coastal town of Flamborough.

While I did see myself as a bit of a wimp on account of doing the route in trainers and not boots, finishing it with only a little ankle soreness was a fillip for my confidence. Of course, I still had the small matter of the forthcoming commando tests, but I'd be fit and refreshed. I was eager to return.

* * *

With no exercise to recover from, 523 Troop had a slight advantage over other troops. Their bodies, like mine, had recovered and we were upbeat for the test week ahead.

First up was the endurance course. I was over the moon when I was pushed into a team with Charlie, as he was my morale crutch and we knew we'd spur each other on.

I needed it. I always struggled on this test. My times were never spectacular. Seventy-one minutes was the time in which we had to complete the course, and I'd finished it in under seventy minutes just the once. I was never going to get a quick time, only a pass time.

But for someone who only wanted to see light at the end of this very long (and wet) tunnel, another chink appeared as I fired the last successful round down the range knowing I had vanquished my greatest adversary. Where I had broken down on the Tarzan assault course three weeks before, I now flew over as if my arse was on fire. As my strongest test, I completed the pass-out in less than ten minutes, one of the quickest in the troop.

On Saturday afternoon, I went ashore with Fred and Charlie a happy man. So happy, in fact, that I didn't buy any green string. That morning, we had run the nine-miler and I'd even pulled someone along, encouraging them to keep up. All there was left to complete was the thirty-miler – again. Even though I'd already passed and didn't need to repeat, finishing the march to be handed the green beret was the best way to receive it.

The big man upstairs must have looked over us with sympathy, as the moor lay resplendent in spring sunshine, flowers swaying to the whispers of the breeze. Light greys of granite stood out proudly from the vivid greens that occasionally darkened under the shadow of a cloud passing across an azure sky.

Navigation was simple, and many checkpoints could be seen from afar. Our syndicate was made up of some the biggest characters in the troop, and as the thirty-miler was, by definition, an endurance test, we made the time go quicker by joke-sharing, poor song choices and the odd comical fall.

Ryder's Hill was still a bitch, but we ascended in cruise control, high on expectation. In just over six hours, we double marched to Cross Furzes. My heart pounded, not just from exertion, but from excitement and pride. There once again stood a line of welcoming commandos, applauding their future brothers.

This time I was to be one of their brethren. This time I had completed the tasks at hand. This time I stood to attention and saluted, before being handed my green beret.

I placed it on my head for the first time. I was no longer 5'6" (and a bit). I was ten feet tall.

\* \* \*

King's Squad is all about promenading around camp wearing a peak cap, drill uniform, white lanyard and contented smile.

We could march smartly around camp knowing recruits would look upon us with awe and wonderment. King's

Squad seemed to be even more respected than the green-bereted commandos around camp. Now I was one of them, I marched smarter than ever before and had an inner lust for life, knowing I'd never have to crawl through those fucking endurance course tunnels again.

Another rite of passage in this last two weeks was to get that elusive tattoo. It wasn't necessarily written in Corps lore that you had to be adorned with ink, but many thought it only right and proper to get something that would make them an obvious target, should they get naked on the streets of West Belfast. The most common, and admittedly the cheapest, option was to get a simple blood group tattoo on the shoulder. Fred had chosen this option.

'I don't want anything too bootneck,' he explained.

'So tell me Fred,' Charlie asked. 'What other groups outside of the military would need to know their blood groups and have them as a tattoo?'

Fred pondered for a while. 'Haemophiliacs.'

This was a fair point, but Charlie was one of a few who thought 'tats' were a bit shit. 'Okay, so why have a tattoo? You've got dog tags to wear around your neck for any medic needing to know your blood group. And what happens if you get your arm with the tattoo blown off?'

'Well, what happens if your neck gets blown off?' retorted Fred, a little quicker than he should have.

My favourite was the classic British bulldog wearing a green beret. Bulldogs have a bad reputation. Noted as the poster dog for right wing nationalism, I couldn't think of a more ridiculous choice to represent our country. Bulldogs, admittedly, are cute as puppies but the term 'bulldog chewing a wasp' wasn't meant as a compliment.

Aesthetics aside, bulldogs often have hip and respiratory problems, can't run particularly quickly over distances longer than a school ruler, and rank seventy-eighth out of eighty breeds when tested for intelligence. Hardly the attributes that a nation aspires to, but as long as it's got the word 'British' in front of it then it's imperialism all the way.

Often surrounded by the words 'Royal Marines Commando' (or 'Pooyal', as displayed on a good friend's arm) the green-bereted bulldog actually looked rather swish, despite the pooch not earning the right to wear it. The tattooist in nearby Exmouth, through locality, had plenty of practice doing this particular piece, unlike the lad who thought his local tattooist in Middlesbrough could conjure up something just as impressive. Unfortunately, the tattooist didn't really understand the difference between a British bulldog and a ferret, which isn't quite so patriotic unless you come from my county.

The problem with getting a tattoo done at the end of training is that many lads have lost weight through the commando phase and are skinnier than usual. Once they pass out and join a commando unit, many hit the weights and grow arms that look better proportioned on a rhinoceros. On such limbs the tattoo metamorphosises from a bulldog with a green lid to a Shetland pony wearing a green duvet on its stretched head.

I sauntered down with intent to see whether there was anything I could scar my underage body with, preferably that didn't consist of military iconography. A black panther eating a snake was rather alluring, unlike the hand swallows many of the miners back home displayed. My personal finances would also dictate my choice: with £10 and a tissue in my pocket, the chances were slim of getting an epic tattoo across the width of my back depicting the battle between David and Goliath, the metaphor for vanquishing my struggles throughout training. So I persuaded the confused tattooist to draw a 'No entry' road sign on my arse, using a paint pot to draw a circle, to warn off anyone at my future commando unit from trying to give me a welcome present I wasn't keen on.

Having a sore arse for a couple of days didn't pose any particular problems in King's Squad. We spent most of our time on the drill square without anything that resembled a weapon, until it was deemed we were to be introduced to the new SA80 rifle brought into general service. But when I say 'resembled a weapon', the initial issue L85 SA80 didn't appear to be a real one.

Based upon the EM2 weapon prototyped in the early 1950s, the SA80 IW (individual weapon) and LSW (light support weapon) were produced in 1975. One would have thought that after nearly a decade of academic research, detailed fine-tuning and stringent testing, they'd have come up with something more useful than tits on a fish.

It was if the R&D guys had gone down to the local MFI furniture store to get ideas on gunsmithing. It was a flat-pack version of a weapon, and came with instructions that needed to be read a hundred times before anyone could make head or tail of them. It had infinitely too many small parts for a general service weapon that could be painfully knelt on. Once assembled, however, it did look good. Yet it was as robust as, well, a flat-pack wardrobe.

Since inception it has caused controversy, and initially its faults were many. Some of the more typical faults we found within the first two weeks of issue were:

The SUSAT optical sight: while exceedingly accurate on a range on a nice summer's day, its glass would mist up as soon as the temperature changed by a degree or a slightly grey cloud came within a mile of the shooter.

The sling: seemingly based on the Rubik's Cube and a spider's web, was an overcomplicated series of straps designed to allow the weapon to be carried in a variety of ways. It was impressive for its aesthetics, but our initial 'ooh', 'aah' and 'that's good' stopped once the novelty turned to realisation that, apart from the default mode of carriage, the other variants were not operationally sound. I can count on one stump how many times I split the sling straps and carried the SA80 down my back; it's certainly not the quickest way to get the muzzle pointed for dispatching outgoing death. To assemble it was bad enough, but should you make a slight mistake and incorrectly thread the buckle the weapon would fall embarrassingly to the floor. It would also crash to the floor should the rubber buttplate at the stock end of the weapon not be secured properly by screws I wouldn't trust on a toilet-roll holder.

The buttplate: made from something resembling green moulding clay, it was so malleable that the rear sling swivel would often be pulled out by the weight of the weapon.

The hand guard: made from a brittle plastic seemingly left

over from when Action Man manufacturers were trying to cut costs.

The magazine release catch: aptly named, every time it would catch on something the magazine would release – usually by accident. It stood out like a racing dog's bollocks; every time the protrusion was knocked, rubbed or given a stern look, it would cause the magazine to fall out of its housing, usually unbeknown to the operator of the weapon. A weapon without a magazine full of ammunition is as much use as an ashtray on a motorbike. At least if you hit anyone around the head with an ashtray, it probably won't break.

The cocking handle: it never stayed where it should have, falling out of its housing and leaving the operator unable to cock the weapon or fire it. Should it actually stay in the weapon, the cocking handle was placed so that it could only be fired from the right shoulder, making firing from certain positions impracticable in an urban environment.

Any excess dirt picked up from biomes such as the desert, tropical jungle, boreal forests, temperate savannah, tropical grasslands, shrublands, any form of tundra or basically anywhere under the sun caused innumerable stoppages, sometimes rendering the weapon inoperable. How lucky would we be to only go to war in a laboratory?

Having been trialled until it had reached an 'acceptable' level, the SA80 weapon system was brought before a committee to rubber stamp it into general service. Stories abound that the committee approved the system's introduction despite knowing of the many faults found in a laboratory environment. Some suggested the upcoming sale of Royal Ordnance expedited the introduction of the weapon, its guaranteed service seen as an attractive proposition to any private investor. Surely such a wilfully irresponsible action would never go on in the corridors of power? Would it?

It's ironic, really, that this new piece of equipment issued to kill the enemy had so many faults it was far more likely to get us killed.

\* \* \*

As well as being shown the world's worst weapon system in King's Squad, we were occasionally taken away for administrative tasks. The most exciting of these was to find out which commando unit we would be drafted to. Unless we were special entry recruits streamed to go on a clerk or chef's course, we had three basic choices:

40 Commando RM – the 'Sunshine Commando'. Never a unit to go to the cold of the Arctic, they preferred Cyprus, Belize, and factor one suntan oil. In the video of 40 Commando, the members of the unit always seemed to have a suntan with a background of beaches. The upcoming year would see them going to Northern Ireland.

42 Commando RM – the 'Pusser's Commando'. Soon to be going to London ceremonial duties. Months of standing in front of Buckingham Palace, Windsor Castle and all the other royal residences looking like garden ornamentation certainly didn't appeal to me. Neither did their seemingly strict regime.

45 Commando RM – the 'Arctic Commando'. Based in Arbroath, Scotland, 45 were much vaunted for their exploits

down in the Falklands. They had not long returned from a Northern Ireland tour and would be going to Norway for three months in the winter. With the reputation of being a brutal unit, I didn't know whether, as a seventeen-year-old bit of skin, my bottom hole would survive, even with my tattoo.

Our drafting preference form gave us three choices. We had been told previously we'd probably get our third choice, the intrinsic value placed on a recruit passing out of training paling into insignificance against experienced commandos due for drafting between units.

With the wisdom of a wise owl, I put down 3 Commando Brigade Air Squadron as my third choice, where the daily operations of assisting the air capability of the Corps translated as playing lots of sport, combing hair in readiness of a night ashore and the occasional bit of work. I knew there wasn't a cat in hell's chance of me going to such a cushy unit.

I put 40 Commando second and 42 Commando first. I didn't like the sound of 42 but I was hoping my gamble would pay off. The personnel responsible for my destiny may have laughed at sending me anywhere other than the unit where I apparently wanted to go to, but unbeknown to them that was actually 40 Commando. Their base in Taunton was the nearest to home, they had suntans and, more importantly, they were going to Northern Ireland the following year. It would be the first opportunity for me to see some action.

I should have done the football pools that week. My cunning bit of trickery ensured a draft to 40 Commando came through. Only two from King's Squad were chosen to go there, much to the dismay of a few lads who had put it down as their first choice. It was at this point that I realised my time with these lads, especially Fred and Charlie, was coming to an end. It filled me with a sadness I'd never encountered before.

The upside of being back trooped so late in training was that I got a second King's Squad piss-up. This time it was in the salubrious surroundings of The Blue Pig, the marines' bar at CTC. As the youngest to pass out, I was given the honour of saying grace before we ate but given a sermon that could only commend me to hell.

Joining me were the strippers who, I have to say, could only be described as filthy. Unlike the old hags in Okehampton, these girls were extremely attractive and showed parts of their anatomy I never even knew existed. They also gave me the opportunity to put my fingers inside a woman for the very first time, and I can honestly say those pubescent years of masturbating like a naughty monkey while experimenting on oranges came in exceedingly useful.

\* \* \*

The only real issue to overcome was the adjutant's inspection. Rumour had it that if we didn't pass he could prevent us from passing out. We didn't know whether this was true or not but we didn't want to find out. We only saw the adjutant when on the drill square and didn't really know what his appointment entailed, apart from giving out extra duties or sitting on a horse that permanently shat all over the square's tarmac. We had seen him throughout training and undergone his inspections twice before. They were always feared, as kit had to be twice as clean, three times as pressed and four times more polished than normal. When inspecting he would ask questions that couldn't properly be answered.

Adjutant: 'How long have you spent on your uniform?'

Recruit 1: 'Three hours, Sir.'

Adjutant: 'Do you think that's long enough?'

Recruit 1, now nervous: 'No, Sir.'

Adjutant: 'So, you don't think my inspection is important? On the flank.'

The adjutant moves along to the next recruit, who has just heard the last conversation.

Adjutant: 'How long have you spent on your uniform?'

Recruit 2: 'Four hours, Sir.'

Adjutant: 'Do you think that's long enough?'

Recruit 2, again nervous: 'Yes, Sir.'

Adjutant: 'Obviously not, you need far longer. On the flank.'

The adjutant moves along again.

Adjutant: 'How long have you spent on your uniform?'

Recruit 3, confident: 'Seventeen hours, Sir.'

Adjutant: 'On the flank.'

On the drill square I was always consistent: consistently picked up, a 100 per cent record of being sent to the flank by the adjutant for my perceived slovenliness. It would have been more efficient for me to parade on the flank at a reserved spot with my name on it. It would have at least cut out the middleman.

But we were nearly there. Our pain and suffering were coming to an end. We had conquered the longest infantry training in the western world and the phrase 'stand by' was a distant, if nightmarish, memory. There was little reason for us to get beasted anymore; we had done everything required. Everything but one thing it seemed – the dreaded mud run.

The Exe Estuary sits at the other side of the Exmouth train line from CTC. It is a site of international importance for wading birds, and of domestic importance for beasting nods.

It had come to the attention of the training team that the troop had yet to do a mud run. Apparently, one of the nods at the King's Squad piss-up was boasting that we had gotten away with it. And we may have done, if it weren't for that boast being within earshot of the troop PTI. But if I were to say we were forced to do a mud run as a punishment for some calamitous indiscretion, I'd be lying. We were just forced to do a mud run.

'On the landings now,' echoed the yell from the landing.

We still ran like the wind into attendance, but as King's Squadders we had every reason to believe we would be addressed politely about some fluffy undertaking, maybe a refitting of our blues uniform prior to our pass-out display, or an opportunity to go into Exmouth as we were nearly trained ranks.

'You cunts think you've already passed out,' shouted the PTI.

I hoped he was going to add, 'so you can all go ashore in Exmouth.'

There was certainly a dislocation of expectation in his voice. 'I have a rule. I will only beast people if they've fucked up. And while you lot haven't fucked up per se, your attitude leaves a lot to be desired. Humility is a great strength for bootnecks, so when I hear you cunts bragging that you haven't done a mud run, there needs to be an attitude adjustment. Get into your bottom field gear and parade three ranks at the bottom of the 30ft ropes. Go!'

Panic overrode any propensity to be scared. We launched as we had done a hundred times before into a quick change. Racing with the energy of not having done any proper exercise in a week, we reached the bottom field – an area we thought we had said goodbye to a long time ago.

At the foot of the ropes were two other PTIs. Neither spoke. It must have been a first. One just rubbed his hands and smiled at us all. His crystal ball was working. Ours was certainly becoming clearer. Our PTI ran past us to the bottom gate, where the marine sentry opened up the gates of Hell.

'On my word of command, three ranks on the mud in front of me. Go!' shouted our PTI rather cheerfully.

If' I'd kept up my geological studies from when I was a schoolboy, I might have been interested in the alluvial deposits. From afar it seemed I was – I had my fucking head in them. As soon as we paraded in the ankle-deep mud the three PTIs let loose. No longer silent, they became a triangle of noise:

'Bend stretch, bend stretch, bend stretch,' shouted the adjacent PTI.

'Roll over, roll over, roll over,' screamed the opposite PTI.

'Ten star jumps go! Ten burpees go!' snarled the hypotenuse PTI.

As we probably all did when back on our PRC, we were doing the wrong thing at the wrong time – every time, according to the diaphragmatic pitch of the PTIs.

Our bodies struggled to sprint. It may have been something to do with the mud now becoming calf deep.

'Oi, you, Lofty, you're not covered in mud, stop loafing,' shouted our PTI whose white vest, if the measuring stick of laziness was the proportion of mud spread over a person's body, suggested he was the laziest fucker of all. It was an observation I didn't really want to convey.

The mud on the Exe Estuary smells as it should – earthy, salty and a bit shitty. It tastes like it smells. There was mud now in every orifice of my body. If I shat my pants at this very moment no one would know. Heaving, wheezing breath echoed in the splattering, energy-sapping mud. Any mud that flew in the eye was impossible to remove – there wasn't anything to wipe our eyes on that hadn't been caked itself.

My flailing, star-jumping arms flicked a globule of mud into my ear. It was like listening into a shell, only it wasn't the sea I could hear, it was the echoing screams of the PTIs still intent on bringing us to our knees, in which they were close to succeeding. Our beasting was taking its toll. Rapid aerobic exercise folded with the excess weight of the mud. While trying to keep my eyes from mud blindness, all I could see were bodies spitting mud, exercising in slow motion, with a distinct lack of sympathy emanating from the PTIs.

'It's mind over matter, fellas,' one shouted.

'We don't mind and you don't matter,' his partner in crime hollered.

Breathing was hard enough without our mouths and noses being clogged with liquefied soil. Sod the endurance course, stuff the thirty-miler – this was the hardest thing I had ever done.

'Keep moving, no one stops on the bottom field,' shouted our PTI as we were divided into three ranks again.

We weren't technically on the bottom field but we kept up our lead-heavy legs, shuffling into a rather pitiful jog on the spot.

'I would hope that this has been a rather enlightening lesson for you, fellas.'

At that moment in time, the only lesson I wanted was how to work a defibrillator.

'Cockiness, arrogance and being a boastful twat will get you nowhere in a commando unit apart from sickbay.'

Sickbay was looking a very inviting place to be at this moment.

His voice softened. 'Take this as a lesson in humility. You are going to be bootnecks. You don't need to show off.'

\* \* \*

The passing-out parade is the day every recruit dreams of when passing through the gates of CTC for the first time.

It had taken me thirty-six weeks, rather than the customary thirty, to get there. This was longer than many recruits, and at times I wished I hadn't alighted from the train at Lympstone Commando on that memorable first day. But I'd gone through the full gamut of emotions a lad of my age could ever experience, alongside people with whom I'd now share a lifetime bond. Only fourteen of us remained who would pass out on 15 May 1987 as Royal Marines Commandos.

Even my mum and stepdad came down to see me pass out. They arrived the night before the parade, smelling of cigarettes as they always did. We took a trip into Exmouth and ate fish and chips which being southern, was of course inferior to the northern version.

Our final morning started like any other, with cleaning the accommodation. This time, there would be only a cursory glance by the training team. Our lockers empty, our baggage full, on the cusp of our greatest achievement there was an emotional vacuum.

The ecstasy of passing out was tinged with the sadness of leaving comrades with whom we'd shared every agonising second. We may never see each other again, our paths similar yet our motivations different. Before marching away to our future we shared our last moments together. For the first time in my life, I felt a lump in my throat from leaving those I truly loved as people.

Dressed in my full lovat uniform, wearing a cap comforter on my head, we hid behind the curtain on the stage of the Falklands Hall. Charlie had hinted that his girlfriend wouldn't be wearing any knickers in the tiered audience gallery. On opening the curtain, the audience applauded the fourteen young men who stood at ease, milking the adulation from the crowd and using their search and scan techniques to try to find an open-legged girl with no knickers.

The crowd had already watched an information video showing us as a new breed of commandos, steely-eyed harbingers of death who dispatched every potential obstacle of Royal Marines training with aplomb. If only they knew.

We were called forward individually to march, to smartly salute the officer commanding Commando Training Wing, then to take off our cap comforters for the last time. The officer then handed over our Holy Grail.

When it was my turn, I felt electric. With applause ringing

in my ears I officially donned the coveted green beret. I was now a commando. A quickly photographed handshake and then I returned to the troop, this time wearing the commando beret and a huge grin.

Quickly changing, as if we had stuffed up, we disappeared back to the accommodation block only to reappear a few minutes later dressed in full blues uniform. Lined up by the gymnasium, we followed the Royal Marines Band playing 'Thunderbirds Are Go'. Never had it sounded so powerful, never had I felt so powerful. I was on Cloud Nine.

As we marched onto the parade ground, my heels dug further into the ground, my arms were straighter than ever and my head was held as high as anyone could manage. The audience of friends and family awaited us. Seamless, perfect and performed a thousand times before, we marched, firing blank shots in time with the music. We performed slick, drilled formations to the fascination of the crowd, before being inspected by the guest of honour. For once I didn't get picked up. He must have been scared; I was now a commando.

As the parade came to an end, the anticipation grew with a knot tightening in my stomach. Finally, the adjutant shouted the most longed-for final stanza to complete our epic poem:

'Royal Marines, to your duties, quick march!'

# EPILOGUE

**G**iven a long weekend prior to deploying to 40 Commando, I decided to go home to see those I hadn't visited for quite a while. My mum and stepdad had moved yet again, but it was of no concern to me, I was visiting the mates I hadn't seen for some time back in my old haunt of Knottingley.

In Knottingley's neighbouring town of Pontefract, the only place to be on a Saturday night is the legendary nightclub Kikos – if you're an underage drinker with a propensity for violence after a couple of shandies, that is. Patrons have been randomly killed there, one man by a group of stiletto-wielding women who managed to shoe him to death.

But it was a place I was familiar with, so I stumbled there with Rick, a dear old friend who was about to embark on his own adventures as a global bum. As Tetley hand-pump bitter was served perfectly all over Pontefract, and therefore tasted like heaven's milk, I accurately calculated we'd both had more than a couple.

A poor simulation of Caribbean plastic palm trees lined the entrance of Kikos, and as we made our way over the sticky carpet to the neon-lit dance floors, the smell of Malibu and vomit hit the nostrils. But Kikos does have a certain protocol that must be followed to the letter. The club had two dance floors, one for residents of Pontefract and one for those from the surrounding towns.

Rick's parents were now living in Pontefract, so we thought their dance floor would be okay. After all, a couple of Pontefract lasses were giving us the eye and as I was a newly-graduated commando, who could blame them?

Trying to dance as if my shoelaces were tied together, doing the 'bootneck shuffle', I succeeded in attracting attention. I don't know if these lads were dance judges or just very parochial guardians of the dance floor, but within five minutes a crowd had descended on me.

I didn't know where the fists were flying from, but I wasn't doing particularly well at fending them off. I did note that Rick also seemed to be doing his best to get beaten up. Drunkenness is a curse in such situations. Though my inebriation dulled the pain, I knew I was getting a proper pasting.

The cavalry arrived in the shape of the bouncers who dragged the two of us out. Into the cool night air I was cast, like the contents of a dustbin, but minus my left shoe.

Or Rick's left shoe, to be exact, as he'd lent me a pair. They were expensive and relatively new, so I was determined to reunite them. The bouncers, however, refused my request to re-enter. There I stood, covered in blood and beer with only one shoe and a moist sock to walk home in. Obviously this didn't meet their dress code.

Luckily, an old schoolmate, Wayne, was leaving the club as I stood there pathetically. I explained my misfortune and as he was a good egg, he happily returned inside to locate my shoe.

'It'll be easy to find,' I said, wiping blood from my mouth. 'It's on the Pontefract dance floor with no one stood in it.'

I waited with Rick at the main entrance, but our attention turned to the noise at the fire exit. Wayne was ejected just as I'd been, but with my shoe in his hand. He'd located it in the place where I suggested, but the same gang that attacked us earlier saw his recovery operation.

Wayne was set upon, but as a rugby prodigy in his youth he managed to hold onto the shoe as if he was about to score the winning cup-final try. The bouncers had seen events unfold and turfed him out as well. He too was battered and bruised, but he had my shoe.

Drunkenness can bring with it many feelings, differing according to what we drink. Vodka, for instance, makes me immensely withdrawn; scrumpy cider makes me do very silly things but turns me into a happy drunk; a certain brand of lager makes me aggressive, no wonder it's nicknamed 'wife beater' (not that I've ever hit my wife – she'd kick the shit out of me); hand-pump bitter makes me very emotional.

So here I was, very emotional, wanting to see Alison.

Alison had been my childhood love from the first moment I saw her in the opposing primary school team at a road safety competition final. I was only ten and she lived a whole 3kms from my house, in the neighbouring village of Ferrybridge. Just seeing her, sat there at an opposite desk answering questions about how to approach a humpbacked bridge, I realised she was the girl of my dreams. But distance can be such a cruel mistress and I sensed I'd never see her again.

Aphrodite showed me compassion, however, and as we entered secondary school we were placed in the same class. Aphrodite is also a bitch sometimes, as she forgot to inform Alison about me. My love affair became a strictly one-way relationship. Her lust was directed towards the older boys, who could get served cigarettes without ID.

After leaving school, our chosen paths couldn't have been more different. I was Forrest Gump and she was Jenny, a pacifist undertaking a sociology degree at Sheffield University. Yet as good mates we stayed close, writing letters often. So close, in fact, that in my drunken stupor I decided to visit her.

I was going to 40 Commando and then to Northern Ireland. I could get shot, killed, or worse, bummed by some crusty old marine. I needed to see her; it might be my last time. I knew where she lived and so trudged off against the better judgment of Rick and Wayne, who much preferred the attention of the nearby burger vendor.

Nowadays, it would probably be called stalking, but back in the good old days you could jump over someone's fence at 2am and throw stones at their window with little comeback.

The sane thing to do would have been to knock on her front door. But I wasn't sane. My much better idea was to go around the back, using all the commando skills of a shopping-trolley collector, fall into a stream full of bramble bushes, rip my cords to shreds, sink to my waist in stinking, algae-infested water, lose the left shoe again, then scramble over the back fence into her garden.

Carefully picking up rocks that would make a sound but not break the window, I threw more and more until at last the upstairs curtains moved. There she was in all her glory, sleepy, with hair stuck up like straw.

There I pathetically stood, looking like the Creature from the Black Lagoon after losing a fight against the really nasty monster from the neighbouring Red Lagoon. She rushed down, and for the next hour I was in bliss at getting my wounds tended to by my 'Alison Nightingale'. But my kind offer of drunken sex was politely declined. She obviously had a hang-up about not sleeping with inebriated bootnecks covered in blood and algae.

I woke up the next morning with a sore head and my virginity intact, but also a feeling of immense excitement. It wasn't even the fact that Alison came down and made me breakfast in a sexy nightie. It was due to the adventure I was now to embark upon.

I said my goodbye to Alison with little emotion; the clarity of a hangover made me realise my closeness to her had now been redirected to those I was about to rejoin. All I had undergone for the last nine months was for this, my first step into the world of a Royal Marines Commando.

From watching my DL lick a glob of false shit from his arse in the shower of the induction block to donning the green beret in the Falklands Hall, the transition from civilian to Royal Marines Commando was now complete, yet my journey had only just begun.

Sporting a huge black eye, with cuts and bruises all over my face, I boarded the train at Leeds looking like I'd already been to war. As I watched the familiar countryside go past my window, I suddenly had a feeling of *déja vu*. I had boarded this same train at the same time exactly eighteen months before, for the journey down to CTC. The British Rail sandwiches hadn't improved but I reflected on how my life had. My outlook had changed beyond recognition and, although I looked from the outside like a battered child, I now looked upon myself as an invincible man.

My mother had not been there when I boarded the train the previous summer. She wasn't there now. It didn't matter. I had a new mother now who watched over me as the train took me to my destiny.

She would look after me through my youth and into my adulthood. She would offer me advice whether I wanted it or not, giving me the freedom to grow yet supporting me when I got it wrong. It was she who showed me the values of courage, determination, unselfishness and humour, yet exposed me to so much more in her advocacy of humility. Unlike my birth mother, she made me accept praise and chastisement in equal measure, driven by the very ethos she instilled in me. She introduced me to the true meaning of friendship, putting me together with strangers and turning them into brothers, many of whom I had yet to meet. My new mother had created me in her own image and knew me as well as I knew myself. She was still there by my side when I reached Taunton, the home of 40 Commando.

I was back with my real mother now: the Royal Marines.

New chapters of my life awaited me. Even with the most vivid imagination, I could never have imagined all the fun and antics the coming years would bring, shared with some of the most outrageous characters ever put on this earth. Encounters that would make up for all the pain suffered for the first seventeen years of my life.

I could not wait.

Read on for an exclusive extract from
Mark Time's hilarious second book,
*Going All the Way*.

# GOING ALL
# THE WAY

*'Royal Marines should be exiled to a desert island with only loose women and alcohol for company, only allowed off in times of national emergency.'*
MARY WHITEHOUSE, SOCIAL ACTIVIST

THOSE FAMILIAR BUTTERFLIES returned, tickling my stomach as they did on my first day of training, when I alighted from the train platform into the sunshine of Taunton – home of 40 Commando Royal Marines.

A picturesque country town and administrative centre for the county of Somerset, Taunton has the air of an overgrown country village; a once-thriving market square, resplendent in council concrete and blooming borders, contrasts with the odd remaining castle keep that ensnares the history buffs.

Taunton has been home to 40 Commando RM since

1983, or more exactly the small outlying village of Norton Fitzwarren. As the name suggests, Norton Manor Camp was once owned by the local gentry; its commanding manor house is now the officers' mess, standing high above the rest of the camp. Its previous role was as a junior leaders' camp for training the British Army's sixteen- and seventeen-year-olds.

To the local thugs these young lads were easy targets, and many young squaddies were beaten up as a result. When 40 Commando RM arrived, the unit was on a ship bound for exercises around the Mediterranean Sea, so a small rear party was given the task of moving the remaining stores, equipment and paperwork from Seaton Barracks in Plymouth to their new Somerset home. As a rear party they were few in number, and the local ruffians thought that a total of forty commandos were now the permanent camp incumbents. Often the odd bootneck visiting town was given a going over, the thugs confident that the other thirty-nine wouldn't seek revenge.

Unbeknown to them, the 40 Commando RM main party had now returned from the Med, and the thugs had seriously miscalculated as 650 commandos had now arrived. When news of these indiscriminate attacks reached the returning members, swathes of marines entered town and meted out swift retribution. It was an honourable alternative to a welcome march, I suppose.

On entering Norton Manor Camp, I thought I'd gone back to the 1950s. The main gate sentry, dressed in full lovat uniform, stood smartly in front of creosoted wooden huts. Accompanied by Jay, a fellow King's Squaddie with whom

I'd passed out of Royal Marines basic training, the guard commander warmly greeted us, checking to confirm we weren't lost and trying to find the local youth club.

A marine walked towards us, his green beret in his well-ironed green denim pocket. From within the confines of the guardroom strode a brute of a man with a much louder voice. In his hand he held a thin cane tipped with a nickel thimble cap, signifying him as the provost sergeant.

Thankfully, his booming words weren't directed at us. 'Oi, Lofty, where's your beret?'

'It's here in my pocket, Colours.' The lad, although clearly a commando, didn't look much older than me.

'Why is it not on your head?'

'I got a no-headdress chit, Colours. I got my head cut open playing rugby.'

'Ah right, hold on there then.' The provost sergeant returned after a short trip back to the guardroom. 'Let me have a look at your chit.'

The young marine took out from his pocket a small piece of paper written by the camp's medical officer, excusing the wearing of headdress.

The provost sergeant examined it carefully. 'Okay, come here.'

The young marine closed in on the provost sergeant who, in one swift movement that belied his size, reached into his pocket, pushed the chit to just below the young man's hairline and stapled it to the marine's forehead.

'Okay, you can wear your chit instead. Now, what do you want?'

Jay and I exchanged glances. Was this how life in a unit was to be? We had heard it'd be pretty relaxed, the fruit of the labours of our training.

The guard commander smiled, pointing us in the direction of the transit accommodation. 'Welcome to 40.'

My nostrils were aroused by the amalgam of desiccated aromas: pollen, dust, sundry wood treatments and forgotten carbolic soap. I walked along the threadbare carpet laid over creaking floorboards and wondered whether this was the dream I'd envisaged. The wooden transit accommodation was sparse, with pre-prepared bedding similar to that I'd been issued at Commando Training Centre for those many elongated months.

With the whole evening spare before reporting to the movements sergeant the next morning, we sat on our beds pondering what we should do. All options, we decided, were too dangerous. Despite being newly qualified commandos, there was nothing more frightening than being in a camp of 650 others. As a result, we dared not venture out any further than the heads, and only then once we'd done a recce to ensure there weren't any green-bereted loons having a piss.

Late in the evening, an RAF corporal joined us. He was to spend a couple of weeks here before moving to more permanent accommodation at a nearby RAF communications detachment. We said little to him, not knowing whether to call him 'Corporal', as we were just out of training, or 'mate', as we were fully-trained dealers of death who laughed in the face of danger (as long as it wasn't the face of a fellow bootneck).

But he had little to say to us, other than to request the

direction of the NAAFI – somewhere we'd considered visiting, although we thought we might get bummed on the way.

We rose early the next morning and, with stomachs hungry from missing the previous night's dinner, decided to go to breakfast. The RAF corporal followed us into the heads wearing his uniform. Jay and I instantly gained stature watching him shave with his jumper on.

'We don't shave with our tops on,' I explained, echoing the words of my drill instructor in the induction fortnight of basic training.

'I don't give a fuck, mate. I'm not a Royal. Who are you again?'

'I'm Mark,' I said, a little more indignantly than warranted. 'If you do that in the regular grots you'll end up with a regimental bath, one that consists of bleach, washing powder and a hard, bristly bru...'

'I know what a "regi" bath is, son,' interjected the corporal. 'Unlike you, I've been in longer than a NAAFI break. When I want advice from you I'll ask for it. Got it?'

Well and truly put in my place, I didn't really want to start my new career on a charge for arguing with an RAF corporal, so I left the debate rather deflated.

I saw him a couple of days later. He had moved temporarily to HQ company accommodation and had somehow lost both his eyebrows.

Welcome to 40 indeed...